The
Ellel
Story

*The story so far
of an unfinished task*

Peter Horrobin

*International Director
of Ellel Ministries*

**Ellel Publications
1998**

Copyright © 1998 Ellel Ministries Limited

A catalogue record for this book is available
from the British Library

ISBN 1 902344 006

Published by
Ellel Ministries Limited
Ellel Grange
Ellel
Lancaster
LA2 0HN
Tel. (0) 1524 751651
Fax. (0) 1524 751738
e-mail: resources@grange.ellel.org.uk
Website: www.ellelministries.org

Printed and bound in Great Britain by
Clays Ltd, St. Ives plc

Distributed in the UK by
New Wine Press, P.O. Box 17, Chichester, PO20 6YB

Contents

3

Objectives of Ellel Ministries

Ellel Ministries is a non-denominational Christian ministry. The work was established in 1986 with the primary purpose of fulfiling Christ's command to preach the Gospel, make disciples and heal the sick in the widest sense. This is achieved through prayer, teaching, preaching, personal ministry to individuals and by training others to be involved in this ministry, especially in their local Churches.

Basis of Faith

God is a Trinity. God the Father loves all people. God the Son, Jesus Christ, is Saviour and Healer, Lord and King. God the Holy Spirit indwells Christians and imparts the dynamic power by which they are enabled to continue Christ's ministry. The Bible is the divinely inspired authority in matters of faith, doctrine and conduct and the basis for teaching.

Foreword

When people first hear of the work of Ellel Ministries, they often ask questions about its history and development. It is not always easy to answer their questions in the time available. This book tells key elements of the story. It will introduce people to the work and tell something of what God has done to bring this ministry into being.

For some, such a short version of what has been a constantly challenging pilgrimage of faith with God - a pilgrimage that has not been without both its hardships and adventures - will be less than satisfactory. But one day the full story will be written. In the meantime we pray that this book will bless those who read it and provide information for those who need it.

The names of most people in the book are their real names, but in the few instances where the first occurrence of a person's name is marked with an asterisk this is not their real name in order to protect their identity.

In writing this Foreword there are many, many people whom I would like to thank for their contribution to the story. But rather than mention any one individual in a book of this nature I would prefer to thank them all for their contribution, however small or great it has been. Every one has been precious, both to us and the Lord, irrespective of whether or not their names are mentioned in the text.

Above all, however, I would want to give thanks and praise to God for the gracious way in which He has directed and sustained the team over twelve years of pioneering together. All of us have been challenged and changed by the experience and even though some of the times have been hard, we would not have missed them for anything!

But the end of this book is not the end of the story! We feel as though it has only just begun. We give thanks for the past and are glad to follow the example of Joshua and the Children of Israel by publishing these pages as *"memorial stones"* to what God has done in the past (Joshua 4:6). But we also stand with Paul in his desire not to dwell on the past, and say with him, *"This one thing I do. Forgetting what is behind and straining towards what is ahead, I press on towards the goal."* (Philippians 3:13-14).

Peter Horrobin
Ellel Grange
September 1998

CHAPTER I

Early Days

Note: *The first two chapters of this book are written in the first person because they are largely my own personal testimony. Thereafter, because there are so many others who have contributed to the story, the text is written in the third person as if a commentator is observing all that happened.*

When It All Began

In January 1987 fifteen brave souls knocked on the doors of Ellel Grange. They were the first people to attend an Ellel Grange Healing Retreat. They, as much as the very nervous team that awaited their arrival, were pioneers. They were putting their lives into the hands of God in an unknown place with a hitherto untried team of people. But even on that very first Healing Retreat God did some remarkable things.

One man had come on the retreat vowing that this was his last hope - it was either God or suicide. God not only turned his life right round to such an extent that he gave up thoughts of suicide, but pains in his legs and the craving for up to 60 cigarettes a day disappeared. Additionally he received a very specific physical healing. His sense of smell, missing for many years, was restored. But he also went away knowing, above anything else, that God loved him.

Another man and his wife, John and Judy Allen, brought their daughter on the second Healing Retreat. She was going through the distress of a painful divorce. Not only did God bring very deep healing to their daughter, but so touched the parents that within twelve months John and Judy had left their former work and become full-time team members, serving God at Ellel Grange as carpenter and caterer until they retired. The uniquely equipped and furnished prayer room at the top of the front tower is John's permanent legacy of thanksgiving to God for what happened at Ellel Grange. He created the room out of the dereliction of a tower ravaged by dry rot. The whole prayer room is in itself a picture of how the healing and restoring power of God can transform devastated lives.

Since those early days the 3-day Healing Retreat has become the corner-stone of the practical healing ministry at each Ellel Centre. Over 400 retreats have now been conducted, providing in-depth help to over 10,000 people. The structure and teaching which is at the heart of each Healing Retreat formed part of the vision, which I had been praying into for nearly ten years before the work started at the end of 1986. But for me the story began many years earlier.

Family Background

I was born in Bolton, Lancashire, in 1943. My elder brother David was already four years of age. Our Christian parents not only taught me the importance of having a personal relationship with Jesus but, by example, demonstrated that life with God could be an adventure and that a day-by-day walk with Him was the only way of life that mattered. I committed my life to Christ as a child and from at least the age of eleven was aware of God's call to be involved in full-time Christian ministry. As a teenager I assumed that one day this would mean ordination. But as the years went by the door to ordination never opened.

At the time of my birth my parents attended an Anglican Church. I was, therefore, baptised as a baby in the Church of England. But a job change for Dad meant that early in life I moved to Blackburn, a town whose football team still attracts my weekly attention in the winter months! There we attended a Presbyterian Church. For Mum and Dad spiritual life was more important than denominational allegiance and so, when they moved, wherever the local body of believers seemed most alive in Christ became our place of worship.

In Blackburn there was little Christian work being done amongst the many boys who lived in the local community of Lammack. Week by week, therefore, our home was turned into a mini-Church as boys responded to the invitation to come to a weekly Bible class. So many came that two classes were needed. I listened every week to my Dad's illustrated talks. I never forgot the lessons learned through my parents' commitment to the cause of evangelism and the sacrifices which they made to tell those boys about Jesus - they really mattered to God. These were strategic and influential years. This home class was later to become one of the primary influences which eventually led to the foundation of Lammack Methodist Church.

When the family moved to Cheam, in Surrey, in 1953, my denominational pilgrimage took me to the Baptists. In this pilgrimage I was learning profound lessons about the Body of Christ. At 16 I was baptised by immersion at Cheam Baptist Church. From King's College School, Wimbledon I went to Oxford University where my college chapel happened to be Christ Church Cathedral. There I experienced a very different style of traditional high Church anglicanism before spending two years sharing accommodation with the lower Church anglican ordinands at Wycliffe Hall Theological College.

During this time I shared regularly in pastoral activities in hospitals and institutions of correction. In later years I was in turn a member of a Baptist Church, a Brethren Assembly, another Baptist Church and, for many years, the Methodist Church, at the same time as having healthy relationships with Christians in all the other main stream denominations.

College and Work

At Oxford I studied chemistry, followed by a year's research in chemical microbiology. During this year the costs of running an old MG forced me into trying to earn some money! While looking for part-time teaching in chemistry at Oxford Polytechnic, I discovered, on a Friday afternoon, that the Building Department were short staffed. A one-day-a-week job was mine for the taking - provided I could start on Monday! Accepting this appointment subsequently led to me being offered a full lectureship at Oxford Polytechnic in Building Science and Mathematics. Two years teaching in Oxford were then followed by three years as a Lecturer at the University of Manchester's Institute of Science and Technology - specialising in Building Science.

At Manchester I began to write and compile textbooks and reference works in Architecture and Building. This eventually led to me leaving the academic life for the world of publishing. As a publisher I specialised in architecture and building and moved to live near Lancaster - a move that would eventually lead to the work of Ellel Ministries being established at Ellel Grange, just south of Lancaster.

At this time I also envisioned and co-authored *The Complete Catalogue of British Cars,* which for twenty years has been a standard reference book of the classic car fraternity. The latest printing, issued at the end of 1997, is advertised by its publishers as *The British Car Bible!*

Personal Pilgrimage and Vision

God used my interest in old cars to sow the seed in my heart of the healing ministry. I had long desired to own an Alvis Speed 20, but never thought I would ever be able to afford to buy one. In 1970, however, I was offered the vandalised remains of a 1933 Alvis Speed 20 Sports Tourer for just £50. I bought it and with typical enthusiasm set about its restoration, only to find that the chassis was bent and, seemingly, beyond repair! Agonisingly, at 4.00am one morning, after a night working in the garage, I realised the awful truth!

But God chose that moment to speak directly to me with the following words, *"Yes, you could straighten the chassis and rebuild the car, but whilst you can rebuild broken cars, I can rebuild broken lives."* It was a word I would never forget.

A few years later I was challenged afresh by the Lord to read the Scriptures again. I began reading consecutively through the Gospels, not quite sure what I was looking for. I was aware, however, that even though I'd been a Christian for many years, and became a regular lay preacher, there was something major missing from my Christian experience. At the end of Mark's Gospel I was arrested by the words, *"Believers will lay their hands on sick people who will get well"* (Mark 16:18). I looked at my hands and realised that I, personally, had nothing to offer anyone and was powerless.

I read on and came to Acts 1:8 where it says *"When the Holy Spirit comes upon you, you will be filled with power and you shall be my witnesses."* Immediately I knew this was the missing dimension in my life. I knew the Lord, and I knew something of the presence and the leading of the Holy Spirit, but, just like the disciples before Pentecost, I had not experienced the power of God which was to come through the indwelling presence of the Holy Spirit. I knew nothing then of what is now much more familiar teaching on Baptism in the Holy Spirit. I read whatever books I could find on the subject. But it was in the privacy of my own heart where I sought the Lord afresh and cried out to Him for that missing dimension to be filled.

A few days later I was awakened in the middle of the night! It seemed as though I was on fire and glowing from head to foot. The Lord whispered deep in my heart, *"It's OK, it's only me"*. Not the most religious of language, but the exact words which were familiar to me from my childhood when one of my parents would come home and call out as they entered the house.

As a child those words spoke of safety and security as the owner of the house was back in residence. That night I was baptised in the Spirit and I knew beyond any shadow of doubt that the owner of the house was in residence as I experienced the reality of Paul's words *"Your body is a temple of the Holy Spirit"* (1 Corinthians 6:19). It was a life-changing moment in my personal pilgrimage.

Not long after this I became Chairman of the local Inter-Church Fellowship. The Roman Catholic member of the group was a remarkable Irish nun who had spent many years in Nigeria as a medical missionary, delivering over ten thousand babies in the process! Now she was caring for people at the other end of life, looking after the St.John of God Hospital, a terminal care hospice. People of all ages and denominational backgrounds would go to Sister Aine, and her close friend and colleague Sister Callistus, for advice and prayer. She was to become a close personal friend and constant supporter and encourager of the work of Ellel Ministries for the rest of her days. As this book was going to press Sister Aine lost her personal battle with cancer and was taken to be with the Lord.

One day Sister Aine rang up and asked for help. She had a lady at the hospital who was very distressed. Sister Aine didn't know what to do with her and asked me to go and pray with them both. When I arrived at the hospital I didn't know what to do either! Twenty years of Church going had not taught me how to bring healing to a distressed and broken person. All the sermons I had ever heard seemed singularly unhelpful when it came to resolving real life issues. As I prayed, however, God gave me a remarkably accurate word of knowledge about this lady's personal situation. It was the key which unlocked the healing process in her life.

When I returned home that night it was very late. But as I walked to my car it was as if God was speaking to me audibly, so clearly was I aware of His voice. *"I want you to spend the rest of your life bringing healing to those in need, and teaching others how to do it."*

God's word was unmistakable. In a moment of time the call that I had been aware of as a child, the revelation I received as I looked at the bent chassis of an old Alvis and now, this clear word from the Lord were all rolled into one and for the first time I knew what my life's work was to be. I was just over thirty years of age and married with two children.

I began to pray into the vision but immediately encountered a problem. I couldn't pray! It was as if heaven had suddenly closed its gates and prayer was no longer possible. After some time of frustration at the situation I eventually came to the end of myself and heard the still small voice of the Father. What God said was to be one of the most challenging things I had ever heard Him say. *"Before I can let you pray into this vision, you need to know that walking with me in obedience may cost you everything you have and everything you are. Are you willing?"*

Scriptures such as *"take up your cross and follow me"* *(Mark 8:34)* suddenly assumed a relevance not formerly experienced. Slowly, step by step, God took me through every area of my life - home, family, possessions, status, reputation, recreations, interests, etc. God did not say I *would* lose any of these, but it was important to know that there was nothing that would come between me and God in being obedient to His call for my life. It was only when the victory had been won in every area that I was at peace and God released me to pray into the vision.

As I prayed, God began to show me the detailed outline of what the work ahead would involve. I saw how a centre would need to be established as a base for the ministry. Then came the structure and organisation of the work, the Healing Retreats and the initial training courses. Most of the major details of what has become known as Ellel Ministries were lived through in vision, thought about and prayed over many years before they actually happened.

CHAPTER 2

From Vision to Reality

What I did not know was that ten years would pass before the vision would become reality. They were to be years of testing, doubt, apprehension, but above all of intercession as day-by-day I brought the vision to God in prayer. I remained committed to believing that establishing a healing centre in the North West of England was God's primary will for my life.

During those years I learned vital lessons in perseverance and endurance - lessons that would stand me in good stead during some of the more testing times that were to come, after the work had started. These were very important years of preparation as I simultaneously pursued my interests in publishing and bookselling in the world of business and my desire to serve God in every way possible.

Vital Lessons

There were also vital lessons to be learned relating to trusting God for his provision in the terms of finances. There were several occasions when God clearly intervened in my business affairs, turning upside down potentially disastrous situations.

I also learned the hard way about the consequences of disobedience. On one occasion I responded positively to the idea for a book from Gordon*, a potential author. When I went to see him, God clearly spoke to me on the doorstep of his house with the words, *"Have nothing to do with this man."* In spite of such a clear word of warning, I went ahead and signed a contract with him because of the amount of money I expected to make out of the project. This act of disobedience led to the most traumatic experience in my business history. Eventually Gordon threatened both my livelihood and my life. The whole saga went on for many months and at its climax the last of seven telegrams received on the same day relayed the chilling words, *"In ten days time you will not exist."*

This was a time of deep repentance and fresh commitment to God. God can use circumstances to bring us back to Him in a new way. I knew I was forgiven and that God was with me, but was there to be any way out of the crisis? The solution, when it came, was dramatic. On the tenth day Gordon's wife telephoned me to say that she thought I should be the first person to hear that her husband had just dropped dead. At that particular moment, as far as Gordon was concerned, I did not exist!

That night I shared what had happened with an elderly saint who had been praying for me throughout the crisis. His response to the news was, *"I know! God told me through my Scripture reading in Isaiah 14 that the oppressor has now ceased and that I didn't need to pray about the situation any more."* I returned home having learned a very deep lesson and also knowing that it was God who had answered the prayers and delivered me from the hands of the oppressor.

Mission England

Over the years my shop in Carnforth became a well-known place of pilgrimage for book-lovers from all over the world. But the shop also became a focus for prayer as, on a monthly basis, thirty or more local Church leaders would gather in this denominationally neutral venue, sitting among piles of second-hand books, to pray for their community.

It was partially as a result of these meetings that I was asked to become Chairman of the local Mission England Committee and take an active part in preparing for the nationwide Billy Graham Crusade in 1984, which became known as *Mission England.*

My major contribution to *Mission England* was the vision God gave me for a new hymn and song book, originally known as *Mission England Praise.* This was later shortened in title, but lengthened in contents, to become the very popular *Mission Praise.* This book, of which I was also one of the compilers, together with its companion volume for younger people called *Junior Praise,* had a significant impact on the Christian music scene in the early eighties and is still in wide use today. Also at this time I served as a National Council Member of the Evangelical Alliance.

Part of my work with Mission England involved organising an annual conference for Pastors and Leaders at Lancaster University. At one of the Lancaster University Conferences I shared the vision I had been nurturing for so many years with the 300 leaders who were present. It was only a pebble dropped into a pond, but the consequences were far-reaching.

Some of the contacts I made through *Mission England* became strategic in the early days of Ellel Grange. The North-West Regional Chairman of *Mission England,* Bishop Bill Flagg, was to become a Trustee and the first Chairman of the Ellel Grange Advisory Board. And Ken Hepworth, one of the Pastors present at that conference, is now the Director of Ellel Grange.

At about this time a group had begun to meet regularly with me to pray into the vision. They were people whom God was also touching with vision for the healing ministry. Their encouragement enabled me to press on in spite of difficulties.

A Significant Meeting

A significant moment in the future work of Ellel Grange came when Trevor Dearing visited Pott Yeats, near Lancaster, in the early eighties. Pott Yeats is a remote farming community where a marquee had been erected on a Christian farm. The congregation at the meetings sat on bales of straw. People came from far and near to hear Trevor speak or be prayed for by him.

At the end of one of the meetings a young Methodist preacher gave a word in tongues. As Trevor gave the interpretation a heavy anointing fell on the place as God spoke into the lives of many different individuals. The word was calling the shepherds to go out and search for the sheep that are lost, the hurting ones, the broken ones, for in these days the darkness is getting darker, but not to be afraid, for as the darkness gets darker so the light of Jesus will shine yet brighter. It was an urgent call to the Body of Christ to show the compassion of Jesus to a broken world.

There were a number of people at that meeting, who did not know each other at the time but who, ultimately, were to join the ministry team at Ellel Grange. For each of them those meetings, and that prophetic word, had been strategic in their personal pilgrimage. For me the word came as a powerful confirmation of the vision God had already given.

The Future Beckons

In 1985 I went to hear John Wimber at Sheffield. On the final evening of the conference there was a call for Leaders to be prayed for. As the Holy Spirit fell on the meeting I was overwhelmed with God's love and sensed Him speaking three words to me - Accepted, Restored and Commissioned. Each word was of particular significance to me, the final word was a clear encouragement from the Lord that the work was about to begin.

I knew, as I returned from Sheffield, that the years of waiting were nearly over. At the age of eleven God had called me into full-time Christian work. At the age of thirty I knew what that work was to be, but it was not until I was forty that the time was right to pursue the vision to its fulfilment. The group of people who met each month to pray became the first (of many, subsequently) Prayer Support Group for Ellel Ministries, not that in those days the word Ellel had even been thought of!

Initially the group's attention was focussed on the soon to be redundant St. John of God Hospital. The Sisters of Our Lady of Apostles, who owned the site, were to put it up for sale. A new purpose built hospice was under construction at Lancaster. Sister Aine and her staff were to move to the new site. Because of the links with Sister Aine, and the excellent chapel in the grounds, it seemed an obvious place for the new healing ministry to be established and I began to draw up detailed plans as to how the buildings could be adapted for a new use.

The selling agents invited tenders for the property from the various parties who were interested in the estate. The group prayed and although they had no money they knew that if the vision was truly of God that He would provide. They put in a tender of £286,000. But even though it was the highest tender received, the governing body of the order rejected the offer. God gave them no peace about accepting it. Instead they were led to accept an alternative offer, believing that this was God's clear leading to them.

I was devastated. For a time my determination faltered. Had I really heard from God? Was the vision anything more than my imagination? But when the group met again for prayer, there was peace. We were praying for the fulfilment of a vision, not just for the acquisition of a particular building, and with one mind we pressed on in prayer, believing that God would yet show us His way forward. None of us knew what God had in store for us just around the corner.

With hindsight it can be seen that for what God had in mind for Ellel Ministries the St. John of God building, and its particular location, were totally unsuitable. The rejection of this offer was one of the more significant, of many, miracles that were to mark the path ahead. It was also a very profound lesson in the ways that God can lead and direct His people!

CHAPTER 3

The Miracle of Ellel Grange

Note: *From this point on the story is told in the third person to reflect the contributions of so many different people to this story of the developing work of Ellel Ministries.*

In autumn 1985 an Estate Agent friend suggested that Peter should visit Ellel Grange. *"It's not for sale",* he said, *"but it will give you an idea of a building that might be suitable for the work. It's just by Exit 33 of the M6."*

Peter set off down the motorway to have a look. It would certainly be convenient for visitors, being so close to a motorway exit. As he entered the grounds he remembered that some six years previously, in 1979, he had visited the building when the estate was sold by the Sandeman family. It had been in their ownership since it was built in 1860. At the auction of contents he had bought some books from the library. The run-down old building had already been sold by the agents for conversion into an up-market health farm.

By 1985 the Ellel Grange Health Hydro, as it was then called, was fully operational. Peter entered the imposing hallway, and, somewhat apprehensively, asked to see the owners - who turned out to be a local land-owner and his physiotherapist daughter. *"I would like to see over the building",* he said, adding rather nervously, *"in case we want to buy it".* His words were greeted with a polite laugh. They graciously showed him the building, now in excellent condition and with an indoor heated swimming pool in the very room from which Peter had bought the books!

What they did not know was that as Peter walked round Ellel Grange God was saying to him,. *"This is the place, claim it for Me!"* God's voice was unmistakable. Peter asked again if it might be for sale. The answer was a firm *"No"*. But they did take down Peter's number.

When he told Sister Aine of the property and where it was located, so close to Exit 33 of the M6, she laughed. With her Irish eyes smiling, she said, *"that sounds about right. That's what Jesus did. He exited at 33!!"*

Three months later the telephone rang. *"Are you still interested in Ellel Grange?"* the voice asked. In a mild state of shock Peter responded, *"Yes, but we have no money!"* Peter shared the news at the next Prayer Support Group. They told him to go and have another look, this time with a larger group of people which was to include Bishop Bill Flagg from Liverpool. The group were of one mind that the place was ideal for the work, but they were overwhelmed by its size and potential. But if this was God ...!

Buying the Grange

Prices were discussed and agreed with the owner's agent. The building itself was to cost £300,000, and the derelict chapel in the grounds, with planning permission for conversion into flats, another £40,000. Then there was Rose Cottage, at £47,500, and finally all the furnishings and contents another £50,000. On top of all this would be the legal charges and essential publicity costs for sharing the vision with the wider Christian community - a sum which eventually reached a further £20,000. The total money needed was £457,500. At that stage they had nothing!

The first task was to gather together enough money to put down a deposit and sign a contract to buy the property. £39,000 was needed by the 28th February 1986. The group felt no freedom at this stage to share the need with anyone other than the fifty or so people who had been attending the Prayer Support Group. They all dug deep into their pockets and on the 28th February they had collectively donated £39,095. God was clearly in charge.

Contracts were signed with great thanksgiving to God and much trepidation. They were originally given until 31st August (six months) to find the rest of the money, but the solicitors acting for both parties eventually determined a further two months would be needed before completion.

This gave two extra months to raise the money, but, perhaps more significantly, it now meant that if Ellel Grange was to become the centre for this new ministry, its purchase would be completed on the 31st October, Halloween, - a night of particular significance in the world of the occult! At that stage no-one appreciated the spiritual significance of a new ministry, that was to have such an impact on stirring up the Church to deal with powers of darkness, being started on that particular date!

As word went out around the region, there were many significant confirmations that this really was God's will. One of the most interesting came from farmer Alec Sayer. Alec and his family farm the land around the south of Ellel Grange. When the building had originally come on the market in 1979 (for the first time since its construction in 1860 as a home for the then Mayor of Liverpool) Alec, who at the time knew nothing about Peter's vision, had stood on the lawns and prayed over the building.

He believed that God had shown him then that Ellel Grange was going to be used for Christian ministry and that there would be tremendous blessing pouring out from the building as it was used for the glory of God. He saw a golden mist, representing God's glory, rolling down the hillside. When the building was sold to become a health farm, Alec was deeply disappointed. He had been so sure about God's word to him. Had he got it all wrong? Had he really heard from God? But he kept on praying.

At that time much of the building had fallen into disrepair. Much work and much expense was needed to bring it back to full use again. The Health Hydro people slowly restored the property, including putting in new showers and toilets to make most of the rooms en-suite. The building was being given new life after nearly half a century of neglect.

When their work was almost done Alec's attention was caught by an article in the local paper about a group that had applied to the local authority for planning permission to use the Grange as a Christian healing centre. Alec got in touch with Peter to find out if it really was true that the Grange was to become a Christian centre.

He was overwhelmed with joy to realise that he really had got it right. His six years of prayer had probably been strategic in ensuring that all the changes that were being made to the building by its new owners would be compatible with its eventual use for the glory of God. None of the major alterations the Hydro made had to be undone.

Confirming the Vision

As the summer of 1986 progressed the vision was shared with the Christian community in the north-west and, where possible, farther afield. The embryonic team went to many different places to share about the work with Churches who had expressed an interest in the healing ministry.

There were some interesting and very confirmatory responses from those who read the first brochure about the work of Ellel Grange. One lady had a vision about the chimneys. She saw thick black smoke pouring out of them. God told her that the smoke represented all the dirt and muck that He was going to clean out of people's lives through the ministry there. In her vision the chimneys were very detailed and specific. She drove all the way to Ellel Grange to compare the real chimneys with those God had shown her. They were exactly the same!

Another couple would take it in turns to either go to the Church prayer meeting or look after the children. On this particular night it was the husband's turn to go. He returned home very excited. At the prayer meeting God had shown him a vision of a building in which God was going to start a healing ministry. As he drew an outline of the building on a piece of paper, his wife had difficulty in containing both her excitement and puzzlement. For she, too, had had a similar vision while her husband was at the meeting. She drew out her building but it looked completely different from his. What was going on?

The following morning they received a letter from Peter, together with an illustrated brochure showing Ellel Grange from several different directions. The husband had been given a picture of the front of the building and his wife had been given the rear! It was an amazing confirmation that God was at the heart of this new ministry.

At the Christian Booksellers Convention at the beginning of 1986 Peter had an appointment with Selwyn Hughes (of CWR) to talk to him about the vision for Ellel Grange. On the day of their appointment Selwyn's personal reading was from Acts 10 and the Holy Spirit quickened to him the verse in which it says *"three men are looking for you"* (v.19). That very morning three men did seek out Selwyn at Blackpool. They also wanted to share with him the burden they had for a healing ministry in the North.

Selwyn felt constrained to put them in touch with Peter. It was the beginning of an important relationship in which the three men became strong supporters of the work. Gordon Clarke, is still a member of the Support and Advisory

Group. Sadly, however, one of them, Stewart Parker, was to pass away very suddenly, even before the purchase of Ellel Grange could be completed, but not before his influence had encouraged a number of people to become involved and support the work. The third person, Geoffrey Jowett, has maintained an interest in the healing ministry.

Later Selwyn Hughes graciously contributed to a short video telling about the vision for Ellel Grange. This video was strategic in helping people who were unable to get to Ellel Grange to see the place for themselves and catch something of the flavour of what God was doing.

Completing the Purchase

When it came to raising the money for the purchase of Ellel Grange, no actual   fund-raising events were held. Prayer and direct giving were the only means used. Funds did, however, come in from some quite surprising sources. One Anglican Bishop who, as a young man, had played tennis on the lawns of Ellel Grange with members of the Sandeman family, sent £3,000. There were many, many small, and often very sacrificial, donations from people whose spirit had been touched by the vision.

Even the National Westminster Bank got involved, by agreeing to advance £500 to the funds for every person who would covenant to give £10 a month over four years. This meant that those who wanted to help, but had no capital of their own, could make a contribution to the purchase price. There was a very generous gift of £50,000 and also some loans that had to be added into the equation, including a mortgage with the Halifax Building Society on Rose Cottage.

As the 31st October approached, both prayer and activity intensified. It is impossible to capture in words the pressure and excitement of those never to be forgotten days. On the very last days even, there were to be some significant gifts.

On the evening of the 30th Peter sat at his desk and totalled up all the gifts and loans that were available. He could hardly believe his eyes when he put on one side of a piece of paper everything that was needed to purchase the properties, together with all the expenses to date, and on the other side all the income that was available from various sources. The income exceeded the expenditure by just £6! God had worked a miracle.

Entering the Land

The very first guests to stay in Ellel Grange were the members of a Vineyard ministry team from California. They were visiting Lancaster for a mini-Conference following one of John Wimber's main UK Conferences. Peter was one of those who was asked to prepare the ministry team for the conference at a series of teaching nights. The visiting team, led by Glen Tottle, used Ellel Grange for bed and breakfast accommodation during the Conference.

Amongst the Vineyard team were Otto and Sharon Bixler. Whilst at Ellel Grange God put the work of Ellel on their hearts. For years to come they prayed for the ministry. They visited Ellel Grange on eight occasions and finally they came as *"missionaries"* to England and joined the team.

Peter's first opportunity to get to know Otto personally was on the edge of the Ellel Grange swimming pool. In order to prepare the pool for their visitors it had been necessary to put the correct chemicals into the water to ensure that it was safe for swimming. Chemicals were poured into the pool from the appropriately labelled container - but it was found to contain diesel oil! Otto and Peter spent many hours together skimming the surface of the pool with old sheets and scrubbing the edge clean! This was one of many practical problems along the way which carried with them more than a hint of spiritual warfare.

Another couple with a strategic role to play in the work were Barry and Jan Jay. Barry and Jan had formerly shared in the running of a Christian Guest House in the Lake District. They were seeking fresh direction from the Lord for their future when a prayer partner shared with them her vision of Barry and Jan welcoming people to a very large building. Then Barry and Jan read one of the very first Newsletters in which the role of Wardens of Ellel Grange was described in those very terms.

They came to a Prayer Support Group meeting and subsequently wrote offering themselves for the job. Their appointment was one of those highly strategic moments in the development of the ministry. Barry and Jan have now had various roles in the work and been at the heart of the ministry ever since. They were an ideal couple to welcome people on the Healing Retreats and training courses. There are a number of people who attended those early meetings of the first Prayer Support Group who are still strategically involved today, some of whom are on the full-time team. Others gradually moved away and still others decided that the work was not for them. Pioneering (as in any field) can be a painful process, requiring as it does unswerving commitment and dedication.

In breaking new ground many barriers have to be overcome spiritually, emotionally and practically. However, in the whirlwind and the storm God will always have His way and, looking back, it can be seen that His purposes have remained firm. Whether their involvement was short or long term, tremendous thanks are due to all those who contributed and helped in the early days.

CHAPTER 4

Welcome, Teach and Heal

The Healing Retreat Programme

During Peter's years of waiting for the vision to be fulfilled, the Lord gave to him the pattern for the Healing Retreats. As he prayed into the concept of inviting twenty or thirty people at once, to receive counselling and personal ministry, God showed him that teaching had to be a very important part of the Healing Retreat programme.

But what should be taught? Peter searched the Gospels in vain to find Jesus's specific teaching on how to heal people! There was none to be found. What he discovered was that Jesus constantly taught about the Kingdom of God and that when Jesus sent the disciples out to heal the sick he told them to teach about the Kingdom also. It seemed that to Jesus living as citizens of the Kingdom of God was the most important thing.

In this context one of the Scriptures that impacted Peter and was to become foundational for the whole of the ministry lies in the middle of Luke's account of the feeding of the five thousand where we read, *"Jesus welcomed the people, taught them about the Kingdom of God and healed those in need."* (Luke 9:11).

For Peter this Scripture spoke with such clarity about three vital aspects of the healing ministry. *Firstly,* that people need to feel the love that is implicit in the word *"welcome"*. Without loving acceptance people are unlikely to listen to what God is saying to them. *Secondly,* that the teaching needs to be primarily about the Kingdom of God and what it means to be a true disciple of the Lord Jesus. For healing and discipleship are very closely linked, and much of Jesus's teaching on the Kingdom requires us to change our lives and live them according to His ways. And *thirdly,* that the healing ministry is most effective in an atmosphere of love that follows the disciplined application of Kingdom principles.

These principles have not changed since the beginning of the work, and wherever the ministry is established the team seeks to follow these same vital steps of welcoming people, teaching them about the Kingdom and bringing healing to those in need. While healing in itself is important, it can also be part of the process of seeking a deeper relationship with God and working out the personal consequences of being a disciple of the Lord Jesus Christ. For others healing can be a sign, encouraging them to walk on with God and apply Kingdom principles to their lives.

Kingdom Principles

The team discovered that one of the most important Kingdom principles which needs to be practised is forgiveness. Jesus stated quite unequivocally *"if you do not forgive men their sins, your Father will not forgive your sins."* (Matthew 6:15). To many people this Scripture comes as something of a shock, and especially for those who are hanging on to much pain and bitterness through not forgiving those who have hurt them. We ask God to forgive us for our sins, but he says to us, *"Do to others as you would have them do to you."* (Luke 6:31). The message is simple and clear - if you want to enjoy the blessings of forgiveness then you must forgive others. Discipleship is not an easy option, but neither was it easy for Jesus to go to the cross that we might be forgiven.

One lady who was crippled by bitterness was heard to say,

"What right has Peter Horrobin to tell me to forgive? I've been bitter for thirty years and I'm not going to waste one of them!" It was only when she faced herself and chose to forgive that God was able to begin an amazing process of healing in her life. He dealt with her deafness and healed her crumbling spine which had been supported by a thick plastic tube completely enclosing her back.

On every retreat the team teach about the need for Jesus to be Lord. And many, many people find salvation for the first time as they realise that the most important part of their healing is that their spirit, which was dead to God because of sin, is born again through the Spirit of God. Some of these people have been involved in Churches all their lives, but it was only when their healing need brought them to a place of personal re-assessment that they realised where they really stood before God!

Every retreat also contains foundational teaching on the need for accepting God as he really is; allowing God to accept us as we are and begin to change us from the inside out; accepting and, even, forgiving ourselves; and, finally, accepting others and forgiving those who have rejected us for a variety reasons. These Kingdom principles are absolutely vital foundational steps towards healing.

Sadly, however, there are some people who turn back at this point. For various reasons they are not willing to let God have His way in their lives by dealing with their heart attitudes, specific sins or the need to forgive others. They want God to heal their symptoms, but they are not willing to change their lives. Sometimes, such people can then become quite negative towards the healing ministry.

Healing Retreats at Ellel Grange would not be possible were it not for the wonderful body of people known as the Associate Counsellors - people who have been trained by the ministry to counsel and bring healing to those in need.

They are volunteers who, without exception, give extensively of their time totally free of charge. Some travel as much as a hundred miles to be involved week after week. Their commitment and sacrificial dedication is truly amazing. Each centre has between fifty and a hundred such people on whom it can draw to staff the Healing Retreats and provide the in-depth personal ministry, which is such a vital ingredient of the Healing Retreat programme. Over the years there has developed a comprehensive guide to procedures which are acceptable and recommended within the work. This is now made available to Associate Counsellors as a manual of good ministry practice.

Many of the Associate Counsellors also get involved in team visits to local Churches or overseas conferences. Some have subsequently joined the team or shared in teaching as Associate Teachers. Many have benefited richly from their experiences, especially when sharing with the Christians in Eastern Europe and Russia or as part of the ministry team on International Conferences.

Even though a normal Healing Retreat lasts for forty-eight hours, spread over three days, the ministry never charges for either personal ministry or for food and accommodation when people come for a Healing Retreat, or for a personal counselling appointment. This is consistent with the pattern the Lord established for the ministry right from its earliest days, when it was clearly understood that the team were to give away to those in need what God had given to them. At each Healing Retreat opportunity is provided for people to make a donation to the work if they wish, but the gifts which are received in this way only cover about a third of the real costs. The rest of the financial support for the work has to come from donations or training course fees.

CHAPTER 5

The Ministry Develops

on and off the base

Training Courses

The first training courses at Ellel Grange were a one-day course entitled *Getting Acquainted with the Healing Ministry* and a residential course entitled *Moving on in the Healing Ministry*. These pioneering events paved the way for a large range of training courses which today embrace subjects as wide ranging as *Ministry to the Childless, Acceptance and Belonging, Deliverance Ministry Training* and *Healing from Emotional Pain*.

As the team has grown in experience they have also grown in their knowledge of how to tackle particular problems in people's lives. It has been possible to structure special training courses so that the team's experience can be shared with others - especially those who have ministry responsibilities in their local Churches. What is taught has always been a fruit of what has been experienced in practice, as the Word of God has been applied in personal ministries to many, many people.

In the early days of the ministry many people came for help who had previously received much counselling and prayer through what is known as inner healing ministry, but they still had their problem. Gradually God showed that, for some of these people, the reason they were no better was that they needed to be delivered from powers of darkness.

Healing Through Deliverance

In the Lord's prayer Jesus encourages us to pray *"Deliver us from evil"* (Matthew 6:13) and throughout the Gospels a significant number of the people that Jesus healed were delivered of demonic spirits. The team learnt that for some people deliverance was, just as in the Gospel accounts, to be a vital part of their healing. But it took somewhat longer to realise that deliverance ministry is much more effective when any 'rights' evil spirits may have in a person's life are first removed.

Deliverance is a normal aspect of Christian healing ministry and is not to be feared. Sensationalising it has been a work of the enemy itself. Over the years the ministry teams have learnt that by undoing the rights demons have to be present in a person's life (through repentance, forgiveness, changes of heart attitude and inner healing, etc), demonic powers have then had to leave quickly without major struggles.

But, as with all learning experiences there is a learning curve and, inevitably, one doesn't get it all right at once. With some of the people whom the team tried to help, in the early days of the ministry, deliverance was attempted prematurely. Whilst it was easy to address the demons and sometimes see them manifest, often they would not leave because there were deeper healing and discipleship needs that needed to be discerned and addressed. The learning curves were frequently steep! But the lessons were learned and some very profound healings began to take place.

Simon*, a man whose marital relationship had become violent and was on the verge of being broken, came with his Pastor for help. This man had already received much counselling ministry, but to no avail. Peter was at a loss as to what more he could do, except for God putting into his head the need to pray a simple prayer, asking God to expose any darkness in Simon's life. Peter did just that and within minutes Simon slipped off the chair in a semi-rigid position and wriggled across the floor! He eventually went through a major deliverance which transformed his life and relationships.

A couple applied for a job at Ellel Grange. They had been childless for eleven years and were beginning to believe that this was God's will for their life. They were certainly suitable for the job they had applied for, but after the interview Peter prayed for them and Pauline was delivered of a spirit of death. Ten days later she was pregnant and nine months later Lucy Anne was born!

Jennifer* was one of the first people to come to Ellel Grange for help, but no matter how hard the team tried they were unable to help her. Demons manifested easily, but they always seemed to be stronger than the faith of those who were praying. Scripturally, however, that cannot be the case, because Jesus has all power and authority and he gave that power and authority to disciples to be exercised in proclaiming the Kingdom, healing the sick and casting out demons (Luke 9:1-2).

Many different things were tried and, inevitably, paths were explored which, with the benefit of further experience can now be seen to have been unnecessary or, even, unwise. But Jennifer realised that those who prayed for her had only one motive - to set her free in Jesus's name and she laughed and cried with them as they sought for answers.

God gave her an unshakeable trust that one day He would provide the answers for her healing at Ellel Grange. Notwithstanding the agony of waiting and the occasional, but unsuccessful, 'let's try again' exploit, she allowed God to test her patience to the limit as she remained committed and loyal, both to God and to those who were doing everything they knew to try to find those vital answers.

Ten years later the answers came as, through ministry to others, profound keys to *"binding up the broken-hearted"* (Isaiah 61:1) were learnt (see Chapter 17), and later applied to the problems Jennifer had experienced. Slowly but surely healing came and the demonic powers had to give way to the authority of Jesus. God rewarded Jennifer's patience and now, with the problems behind her and a life made whole by Jesus, she is giving back to the Body of Christ by reaching out herself to hurting sheep as she shares with them what Jesus has done for her.

A Church that ministers healing will always have people with a story to tell about what God has done. At its heart that is what evangelism is - telling others what God has done. A healing Church will, almost automatically, become an evangelising Church.

In the healing ministry one sees considerable relevance of the Scripture that says *"my people are destroyed for lack of knowledge"* (Hosea 4:6), for so often it is only when knowledge of the right keys is known and applied that healing and deliverance comes. Paul may have said to the Corinthians *"knowledge will pass away"* (1 Corinthians 13:8), but for the time being we still live in the flesh and Godly knowledge is vital for mankind's well-being.

The wrestling with those demonic forces, which had such deep holds in some people's lives, often went beyond the current experience of the team. A very deep trust in God was needed to walk the path of obedience that led to such people being set free, not to mention the hundreds of hours of intercession and prayer ministry. These were some of the most holy and precious times, when on a daily basis, the application of the work of the Cross brought forth such wonderful fruit in the lives of the hurting and broken.

These occasions led the team to an unshakeable reliance and trust in God's protection as they were given a deep understanding of, and an unswerving belief in the truth of Scripture. They saw God's heart. The cost and sacrifice that such long ministries entailed was enormous, but the outcome and fruit has been pure gold - both for the individuals involved and for the Body of Christ. Wherever the team teach the lessons that have been learned, there is a ready acceptance of the reality of what is taught. The world really is crying out for answers.

When the first *Deliverance Ministry Training Course* was announced at Ellel Grange for October 1987, there were some very mixed reactions from the Christian community. At one end of the scale were those, already involved in the healing ministry, who realised through their own experience that this was a vital area of ministry in which they needed training. At the other end of the scale were those who began to distance themselves from Ellel Grange, even though the reality and fruit of the ministry was undeniable. Whilst no-one could deny the fact that in the Gospels Jesus is described as frequently casting evil spirits out of people, it seemed as though the idea of doing this today was more than some people wanted to acknowledge.

There was, of course, opposition from the more liberal theologians who say that Jesus only believed in demons because he was a man of his day, and that he, like others of his time, accounted for what could not be explained rationally by saying it was demonic. Now, they say, with the advances of medical science, we can see, as people of our day, that what Jesus and others formerly thought was demonic can be accounted for by more sensible scientific explanations. What such comments can't explain, however, is how it is that by casting out demons and bringing deep healing to the broken, people get healed!

There was also opposition from a very vocal and much more conservative sector of the Christian community who certainly believed in the reality of demons, but were adamant that no Christian could have one! Again, it is hard to explain how the lives of mature Christians can have been transformed and healed through deliverance if it is not possible for Christians to have a demon!

Another theologian, who also had a training in psychiatry, said that what Ellel Grange referred to as deliverance was in fact the release of a *"Whoosh of guilt!"* It is perhaps a little harder to provide Scriptural grounds for a whoosh of guilt than it is for deliverance from demons!

How easy it is to refuse to believe or ignore the facts when blinded by preconceived theological or psychological misperceptions! The blind man said, *"One thing I do know, I was blind but now I see,"* (John 9:25), when asked about what Jesus had done. Similarly today there are many who have received deliverance who are equally able to say, *"Once I was bound, and now I am free."*

It seems that this particular battle, over whether or not Christians can be in need of deliverance, has now largely been won. Most Christian leaders would now recognise, almost without question, the necessity and importance of deliverance, as part of the healing ministry. Those Christians who are used to working in cultures which are much more conscious of the spiritual realms struggle to understand how Christian leaders in the west could ever have been so naive as to question the need for the deliverance ministry!

But any ministry that is taking ground from the enemy in the lives of believers is bound to experience opposition. Satan does not give up his territory lightly. Whilst deliverance has always only been a part, though a very important part, of the overall healing ministry at Ellel Grange, it was this area that attracted the greatest attention and upon which critics and the media began to focus their interest in apparent attempts to undermine the ministry.

Pressing on with the Task

One of the lessons that Peter had learnt well during his ten years of waiting was to keep on doing what God had given him to do and not to be diverted from his calling. Ellel Grange continued to do what God had called it into being for and people continued to be blessed as lives were transformed on the healing retreats and the training courses.

These were not academic courses where people only accumulated knowledge, they were dynamic courses in which God was dealing with people as they learned. Indeed, the training courses were becoming a very effective secondary means of ministering to people. Every training course was planned to have a ministry night so that the lessons that were learnt on the course could be applied in the lives of those who attended. There were some very remarkable experiences as, on course after course, the Teachers and Associate Counsellors put the teaching into practice.

One Anglican Vicar learned in the afternoon about the spiritual dangers of freemasonry. In the evening he was set free from powers of darkness. He was astonished at what happened when he was delivered, but went home rejoicing to experience a freedom in his ministry that previously had eluded him.

A lady had come to Ellel Grange with her contoured plastic bed to protect her damaged spine from pain as she slept. She was unhealed after falling down stairs many years previously. She received deliverance and healing ministry and was set free from generational curses. She no longer needed the plastic bed.

Another lady had understood for the first time about the consequences of sexual sin. She repented over things in her life that had taken place seventeen years previously. Not only was she delivered, but she was dramatically healed of epilepsy. Within a short time, with her doctor's cooperation, she was off all medication. Previously she had required the maximum possible dosages of anti-epileptic drugs.

Ministry Courses

A more recent development in the pattern of training courses is the introduction of what are referred to as Ministry Courses. On these there are always a number of team members and Associate Counsellors at hand. The objective of these is both to teach and minister into a specific condition throughout the length of the course. The effect of such courses has been profound, with many people reporting major things that God did for them. Topics covered on Ministry Courses range from *Freedom from Backache* to *Ministry to the Childless.*

Modular Training

Chapter 14 catalogues the development of the 9-week training school. However, such a school, attractive though it may be in theory, is not a practical option for many people. They can manage to get away for weekends on a regular basis but leaving the family or getting time off work for longer periods of time is impossible.

For them especially, Ellel Ministries developed a Modular Training School in which the primary teaching elements of the first part of the longer schools can be absorbed in a series of short courses. On these courses additional personal support and tutoring is provided by the Ellel Staff. At the end of the formal training courses, it is then possible to progress further with the more practical side of modular training by sharing with Staff and Associate Counsellors on Healing Retreats or Ministry Courses.

Church Visits

Ellel has always been committed to supporting and encouraging the work of local Churches and Church leaders. Specially tailored training weekends in the local environment have formed an important part of the overall programme. Many people find it hard to go away for personal or family reasons. Others simply cannot afford the cost of travelling and/or the course. An alternative, therefore, has always been to take the teaching to the Church. In this way the whole congregation can benefit from the teaching and ministry and not just those who are able to afford travel to courses.

This has been an especially attractive alternative when the local Church leaders have been keen to develop an understanding of the healing ministry in the Church as part of a programme of expanding the counselling and healing ministry in the fellowship. The programme of a Church visit generally provides a comprehensive overview of the healing ministry.

A weekend course may, for example, begin on the Friday evening with an introduction to the subject and to foundational theology, followed by a Saturday morning session on inner healing and a Saturday afternoon session on healing through deliverance. The Saturday evening meeting is usually a teaching and healing service where those who wish to can receive personal prayer and ministry. The weekend then concludes with the team's involvement in the Sunday morning services and there is often an Open Forum on the Sunday afternoon to conclude the weekend's programme.

Because basic Christian doctrine, and foundational teaching on the cross, is presented in a more extensive, practical and relevant way than is sometimes possible in the normal local Church service, it is not unusual to find that over a Church weekend a significant number of people come to faith in Christ. Healing and evangelism are closely linked and it is impossible to teach effectively on healing without people having to consider afresh the nature of their personal relationship with God. So the Gospel is proclaimed!

On some occasions the team has made several visits to a Church over a period of time, providing a logical sequence of teaching which has enabled the whole fellowship to move forward together. This has then led to some members of the Church visiting one of the centres for more specialised training, which they can then take back and use in the local Church ministry team. Increasingly members of local Church ministry teams are choosing to come on the Modular or one of the residential schools, as this is a very effective way of both going deeper into God for themselves and a preparation for them to be able to help with more in-depth ministries in the home situation.

Claiming the Ground

When Ellel Grange was first acquired a special time of thanksgiving took place as the building was dedicated to God for the ministry that lay ahead. At that time the leaders were not as aware of the need for cleansing before dedication as they are now. But as the months went by, and God brought different people to the Grange for help, some of them, because of the experiences they had gone through in life, were found to be particularly vulnerable to powers of darkness - especially, in some cases, demonic spirits that seemed to be resident in the building.

The derelict chapel in the grounds seemed particularly attractive to those who were suffering severe demonic oppression. Some found it very hard to stay away from the building. It was known, however, that the derelict building had been used in the past for occult practices so it was not surprising that some people should be drawn there.

On the day that the team chose to address whatever powers were affecting the chapel the weather was sunny with clear blue skies. As they lifted their voices in praise to God and came to the point of dealing with the demonic powers, the weather very suddenly changed. A heavy black cloud came, it seemed from nowhere, and torrential rain was blown through the open windows by high winds. Almost as quickly as this sudden and violent weather arrived, it went, as the team pressed on in praise to Jesus, proclaiming His Lordship over the place.

This was all part of learning to understand about spiritual warfare. For what they found was that now, as owners of Ellel Grange, they had authority to acknowledge the sins of those who had used the building in the past and cleanse the property of any demonic powers that had been given rights through the sins of previous occupants and owners. These were profound lessons as the Lord showed step by step those things that needed to be prayed about.

One of the biggest steps forward was when the team forgave all those in the past who had been involved in freemasonry. A number of people who, prior to that, had been oppressed by demons in the building felt safe from that moment on. Other rooms in the building needed cleansing from spirits associated with unclean sexual activity and, in some cases, other occult or New Age practices.

In 2 Chronicles 29, King Hezekiah gave the Priests instructions on how to cleanse the temple which had been desecrated in the reign of his father King Ahaz. First the Priests had to cleanse themselves and then they had to cleanse the temple before it could be dedicated afresh to the Lord.

Teaching based on this principle, and illustrated with the extensive experience the team gained as they subsequently prayed in many Churches and buildings, was built into a special training course called *Claiming the Ground.* Churches reported significantly different spiritual environments as they put the lessons into practice. These lessons were to prove absolutely vital in later years as the work expanded and other centres were brought into the ministry.

After a few years of experiencing God move so powerfully at Ellel Grange, it was not surprising that news of what God was doing in the north-west of England was spreading to other regions. Many people on the courses were from the south of England and gradually the Lord was impressing on the leadership the need for an Ellel Centre at the other end of the country. But before that could happen the team were to head for Brighton for *The Battle Belongs to the Lord!*

CHAPTER 6

The Battle Belongs to the Lord
The First Brighton Conference

Whilst God had been blessing the ministry at Ellel Grange abundantly, the work was largely unknown in the wider Christian community. Some people began to encourage the team to take the ministry to a larger audience and put together a national teaching conference. But would people go to hear an unknown group of home-grown speakers?

But then Bill Subritzky came to the United Kingdom. Bill is a larger than life New Zealand Anglican - an ex-lawyer with an incisive word of knowledge ministry and much experience of healing and deliverance. Chris Mungeam, the Managing Director of the publishers Sovereign World, and with whom Peter had been a fellow Church member in his youth at Cheam Baptist Church, was Bill's publisher in the UK. Chris later became the publisher of Peter's two books on *Healing Through Deliverance* and for a period of time both he and his wife Jan served as Trustees of the work.

Chris introduced Bill Subritzky to Ellel Grange. Bill made a preliminary visit to England to explore possibilities. Derek Prince, an old friend of Bill's lent his support. A programme was put together called *The Battle Belongs to the Lord*. Peter Horrobin, and another Sovereign World author, Graham Powell, were to be the other speakers.

The publicity for *"The Battle"* went out far and wide and the bookings also came in from far and wide, including many from overseas. It seems that the contents of that first Ellel conference struck the right chord for where the Church was at in 1990. There were many testimonies of healing and many people came to the Lord. For many it was the first time they had seen the reality of healing through deliverance - especially as modelled by the speakers.

It was a conference that was to change the nature of Ellel Grange from being a parochial ministry for the North West of England to being a ministry with a much wider national and international potential. Invitations began to flow in from overseas, as well as much farther afield within the UK.

One person who was deeply challenged was Chua Wee Hian, now the Pastor of the Emmanuel Evangelical Church in London which meets at the Emmanuel Centre in Marsham Street, Westminster. Wee Hian had a lifetime of evangelism and teaching experience and had exercised a world-wide ministry as General Secretary of the *International Fellowship of Evangelical Students.*

Wee Hian's son Steve was about to be married. He had just completed his theological training at Aberdeen University where he had met Barb, who was studying there after completing her degree in the USA. Steve and his wife-to-be were wondering what they would be doing together after their marriage. Another opportunity for Christian service in the States did not materialise and, following the conference, Wee Hian contacted Ellel Grange to see if there were any vacancies on the Young People's Service Team.

There were, and Steve and Barb were welcomed with open arms. The need for young people was great, and even though they came with some trepidation, they threw themselves into their tasks with considerable skill and enthusiasm. God not only blessed the work through them, but Steve, especially, was deeply healed by the Lord also. Steve's musical skills quickly came to the fore and now, seven years later he is the international worship leader of Ellel Ministries and the Assistant Director of Ellel Canada.

He and Barb are growing a young family in the work. Their children, Joshua and Hannah, are important members of the team - as are the children of all other team members.

Jill Southern came to *The Battle Belongs to the Lord* because she was desperate. Fear controlled her life and no-one seemed to have any answers. She heard that there would be teaching on deliverance at the conference. She didn't know what that was but someone had told her it might help! So she went, almost as a last resort.

After one of Bill Subritzky's teaching sessions she was ministered to by one of the elderly Associate Counsellors from Ellel Grange. Both were equally astonished to see what God did. Jill returned home a different woman. The story of her healing is told more fully in the June 1998 edition of *Renewal Magazine*.

Later, Jill, who was then an Executive Director with Thorn EMI Computeraid, was to attend the second 9-week *School of Evangelism, Healing and Deliverance* at Glyndley Manor. She is now the Director of Ellel Pierrepont. God's leading in her life and how she became involved full-time with Ellel Ministries is a story in itself.

Chris Leage, then the National Leader of the Lydia Fellowship, was also at Brighton. She and a team of other Lydia intercessors provided continuous prayer support throughout the conference. But Chris's friend was also unable to conceive a child until, that is, she was prayed for at the conference. Shortly after the conference a child was conceived and nine months later Daniel was born. She had been told by doctors that she would not be able to conceive.

Even now fresh testimonies of what God did through that original conference continue to surface from time to time, although nearly ten years have passed since those memorable Brighton days when 3000 people filled the Brighton Centre. Only recently a man came running up to

Peter, put his arms round his neck and kissed him on both cheeks! *"Thank you,"* he said, *"for what God did for me, my family and my Church through The Battle Belongs to the Lord. All have been dramatically changed"*.

The following year the same teaching team were back in Brighton to teach *The Battle Belongs to the Lord* again. This conference was being run simultaneously with the development of major new projects which were to extend the work of Ellel Grange from its north-western roots to Glyndley Manor, near Eastbourne, in the south of England and, even farther afield, into Eastern Europe!

Since then the team have taken *The Battle Belongs to the Lord* Conference to many different places. Wherever this vital material has been taught there has been tremendous fruit as the Holy Spirit has anointed the teaching and brought great blessing into the lives of many people.

Not only does the programme introduce people to the whole subject of healing but more recently the foundational teaching on basic Christian truth has been strengthened and extended within the original conference programme. As a result a senior leader from the United States was heard to say that one of the more important aspects of Ellel's teaching at *The Battle Belongs to the Lord* is that it unites Churches in their doctrine and not just in experience!

To date *The Battle* has been conducted in the following locations: Brighton - England (twice), Budapest - Hungary, Kuala Lumpur - Malaysia, Kota Kinabalu, Sabah - Malaysia, Hong Kong, Weinfelden - Switzerland, Toronto - Canada, Orangeville - Canada, Atlanta - USA, Kremenchug - Ukraine, Wroclaw - Poland, St.Petersburg - Russia.

CHAPTER 7

Young Peoples Service Teams

Part of the original vision for the work included a team of young people who would give a year of their life to the Lord, serving Him in the practical duties of the work. The YPSTs, or YIPS, as YPSTs is normally pronounced, have truly been the lifeblood of each centre. Without them the ministry could not have functioned.

But it has not just been a one-way process of benefit. For many of the young people their time with Ellel has been life changing. They have had the opportunity of being on the sharp-end of a pioneer ministry and seen for themselves the power of God at work transforming people's lives.

Not only have they served in essential duties such as preparing food, making beds and cleaning toilets, but they have also formed the music groups, supported others in counselling ministry, run the bookshop, been part of ministry teams on Church Visits up and down the country, gone on overseas trips to Eastern Europe, sat in on training courses, operated the sound desks at healing retreats, training courses and conferences and, above all, had the opportunity of being enriched by challenging Christian fellowship at a very strategic time in their lives.

On the practical side of things, Ellel provides free living, accommodation and food and also gives each YIP a small weekly allowance. Most find this adequate to live on, though some do have the benefit of additional support from their local Church, parents or friends back home.

Some YIPS have found their life's calling while at Ellel. A significantly high percentage go on to some form of full-time Christian work. Having shared in the reality of Kingdom life, and seen God powerfully at work in so many people their eyes are opened to the potential their lives have for God. At Ellel Centres they share in both the joys and the pressures - they learn something of the reality of what Christian work is all about.

They are also challenged personally in areas of Christian living. When they hear people giving their testimonies on Healing Retreats they learn first hand some of the consequences of not living a Godly life, as well as what God can do to bring restoration. The lessons are learned by example as well as through teaching. They also learn the importance of discipline and servant-heartedness through the routines of the ministry. Many adults who have visited the Grange have bemoaned the fact that they did not have a similar opportunity when they were young!

Some YIPS come to Ellel by way of taking a year out between school and university, or school and some other form of further training. Others have done a similar thing after leaving college and before getting a job. Some have deliberately come because they know God has called them into Christian service and they wish to get some experience while waiting God's opportunity for them. A number come from overseas - for them it is an ideal opportunity to develop their English language skills as well as to mature in a Christian environment away from home. Even for those who come for a year, and then move on to something completely different, the opportunity of serving the Lord in a disciplined Christian atmosphere is a strategic influence on their lives for good.

Now that there are a number of different Ellel Centres, YIPS can do a second year, if they wish, at another centre where they are able to take a more responsible role because of the experience they have already had. Having served the

Lord in many different aspects of the work their in-depth understanding of the ministry equips them to grow quickly - both in usefulness and effectiveness - as some of the following stories illustrate. Most importantly they find themselves in God and can begin to fulfil their potential as men and women.

Chrissie was the very first YIP. She was a character in need of an opportunity! God used her time at Ellel to do a deep and steadying work in her life - a work which has born rich fruit in the succeeding years. Now, ten years later, she is married with a two year old daughter. She and her husband have joined the team together at Ellel Grange and her parents are Associate Counsellors.

Elaine was in marketing with a Kendal shoe company. The challenge of selling shoes for the rest of her life was less than attractive to a girl with lots of energy and gifting. She gave up the good money she was earning in shoes for a YIPS allowance. She not only found an opportunity for service, but God also began to show her the areas in her life where He needed to do a work of healing. She later met and married Mark East, then a young curate and also the son of Reg East, whose pioneering work in the healing ministry is so well known. As well as being a Vicar's wife in a busy Midlands parish, she works for a local charity helping the elderly and disabled.

Pete was a Yorkshire lad with a great sense of humour and a natural enthusiasm for God. His time at Ellel was formative in helping him to see what were to be his priorities in life. He is now working as a project leader on a farm for rehabilitation of young offenders after serving some years as Assistant Pastor in a Baptist Church.

Cath took a year out after leaving college. She was trained as a secretary but had little opportunity to use her secretarial skills during her year as a YIP. There were much more fundamental things that needed doing! But during her last weeks as a YIP, only days prior to leaving, she went on a Church weekend to Wales. At the end of the weekend Peter ministered to two young ladies who had suffered lifetime consequences of a car accident as children. Peter asked Cath to make a note of what was happening in case there was to be any follow-up ministry at a later date.

Cath recorded everything that happened in short-hand. It was the first time she had come face to face with the reality of actually seeing God transform a person's life through healing. Later she transcribed her short-hand into an excellent set of ministry notes. She changed her mind about leaving and decided to do another year in the ministry. During that year she met and fell in love with Andy.

Andy came into the work by a slightly different route. He was at University, and for his Business Studies degree he had to take a year out in some form of industry to study marketing. He came from Gold Hill Baptist Church where some of the members had had contact with Ellel. He asked if he could do his year at Ellel Grange! During that year he produced a report on Ellel's Mail Order Department that was sufficient for him to get a good degree. But, more importantly, God also used him to support the Leadership with some in-depth ministries. What he saw God do changed the whole direction of his life - he also fell in love with Cath!

Andy and Cath were married at Ellel Grange in July 1995. For three years Cath was Secretary to Peter and the Executive Leadership. And after two years putting his degree to good use in charge of publicity, Andy is now responsible for administrating Overseas Development within the work and is Peter's assistant. Following the birth of their first child, Jacob Daniel now occupies most of Cath's time!

The story is told elsewhere of how Steve and Barb Chua joined the YIPS at Ellel Grange straight from their honeymoon! Living in one room in the middle of a young people's house was quite a challenge at the beginning of their marriage. But they applied themselves with servant-hearted diligence to all the tasks they were given and during that year Steve's musical gifting also began to develop. Barb's administrative skills were put to good use in, amongst many other things, compiling the team manual on how to run a major conference and as the first Secretary and Administrator for the Trustees and the developing Executive Leadership.

They stayed on in the work at Ellel Grange as Youth Pastors and trainee leaders, as well as overseas pioneers, especially to Steve's native Chinese communities of East Asia. Steve's primary role for a two-year period, however, was as Personal Assistant to Peter. In this position he had ample opportunity to see the work first hand and in close-up. This gave him a much wider perspective on what God was doing on a world-wide basis through the ministry and equipped Steve and Barb to be ready for fresh challenges, as and when God opened the way. It also gave them experience of learning to walk in obedience to God, whatever the superficial circumstances may seem to be.

The developing situation in Canada then proved an ideal place for them to go and develop their leadership, management and teaching skills, alongside the then Executive Director of Ellel Canada, Ken Hepworth. Ken is now back in England as Director of Ellel Grange. Donna Parachin is now the Executive Director of Ellel Canada with Steve as her Assistant Director.

In 1992 a small team went to the Ukraine following the conference in Budapest. Some of them stayed in Sasha's home. Three years later Sasha applied to Ellel Grange to serve as a YIP, like many other Eastern Europeans have done. At the end of his year in England he chose to do another year in Canada. Musically Sasha is an able drummer, but he is also a fluent linguist in at least five languages.

Karen came to help with the washing-up for six weeks during her summer holidays in 1987. She is still at Ellel Grange, but no longer doing the washing-up! She so enjoyed her time with the team that she stayed on as a YIP. Her sensitive key-board playing and worship leading was a great blessing on Healing Retreats and she began to develop very special ministry skills in encouraging hurting and broken people who were going through difficult times.

She spent a while serving on the pioneer team at Ellel Canada and has visited Eastern Europe on several occasions to help Otto and Sharon with their work in Hungary and beyond. She now has a very responsible role within the ministry as the human link between the home base and the established overseas ministries - especially Eastern Europe. She also looks after all the travel arrangements for the whole team. It was Karen's continued presence at Ellel Grange that helped both her Aunt and her mother persevere to receive significant prayer counselling and healing ministry. There are many people who have good reason to give thanks to God for her sweet influence on their life.

Most recently she has just produced an excellent and very sensitive collection of songs on a new cassette called *"Love in His Eyes"*. This was compiled with Steve Wright, another of the YIPs who served at Ellel Grange in the early days. The songs are all written and sung by Karen and Steve. They will minister deeply into the lives of the hurting and wounded.

Gareth joined the team lacking confidence and with little idea of his giftings and abilities. When he eventually moved to other employment he was married, had become a very competent guitarist and worship leader as well as understanding some of the complexities of sound engineering.

Christine Ernst was the first YIP from continental Europe. She has consistently prayed for the work of Ellel in her native Germany and now, seven years later, she is seeing the fruit of her prayers coming to pass as doors are opening to the German speaking peoples. She now serves the work in middle management and is an extremely loyal and valuable member of the team.

Lindsey Stanier is unique amongst British YIPS in that she has served at all three UK Centres. Not only has she given her all to the ministry during these periods of service, but she also discovered that she had a natural gifting in the area of sound systems. As a result she decided to go off to college for two years to train in sound engineering. She, like many others, discovered that while she gave her time to serve the Lord, He answered their prayers for guidance and gave them direction for life.

Whilst not every YIP has been as blessed as those described above, it is true to say that those who have had a negative experience are very, very few in number. One or two left before their year was up. But even some of these came back at a later time and thanked the staff for the godly influence their time at Ellel had been on their lives. Hindsight can be a wonderful teacher!

The above stories are only a handful of those that could have been told. Many YIPS remained to serve the Lord within the ministry for varying periods of time. Others went back to serve their local Churches. Some on to further training, other types of Christian work, or to start a career in their chosen profession. Many, many more stories could be told of how young people joined the teams at the various

Ellel Centres, and God used this time to build a solid and Christlike foundation into their lives.

Serving as a YIP provides a tremendous opportunity to meet and work with people from all over the world, learning about and understanding something of the wider work of the Body of Christ, far beyond the limitations of their local situation. The YIPS often make strong and lasting friendships and have gone on to travel the world as a result! We are tremendously grateful to every young person who has served the Lord with Ellel Ministries. Undoubtedly, without them, the ministry could not have become what it is today.

To date more than 300 YIPS have played their part within Ellel Ministries from over 30 different nations: Australia, Austria, Canada, Czech Republic, Denmark, England, Finland, France, Germany, Hungary, India, Ireland (North and South), Israel, Lithuania, Malaysia, Netherlands, New Zealand, Norway, Poland, Romania, Russia, Scotland, Singapore, Slovakia, South Africa, Sweden, Tanzania, Uganda, Ukraine, Wales, Zambia and Zimbabwe.

CHAPTER 8

Associate Counsellors

The Salt of the Earth

Long before Ellel Grange had been acquired, the role that Associate Counsellors were to play in the ministry was well established in the vision. Not only would they be a vital part of the whole work, but as a team of mature people drawn from many different Churches, they would be a strong protection against the exclusivity and extremism that has sometimes been the hallmark of independent Christian groups. It would also guarantee Ellel's commitment to being a non-denominational ministry.

These men and women proved to be the absolute salt of the earth - totally committed to God and willing to lay down their lives for hour after hour, day after day and, sometimes, week after week on behalf of the hurting and broken individuals who found their way to the doors of Ellel Grange. They were never afraid to say what they thought, call a spade a spade or tell Peter, or any other of the Leaders, if they thought there was something wrong, or God was saying something to them for the team.

None of them were perfect - most came with their own spiritual limps - nor were they superspiritual people with a religious answer to every problem! They were real people, often with the most amazing sense of humour, who responded to an unusual call to join the work of Ellel Ministries as Associate Counsellors.

With people like Edwin Bibby, Bobby and Grace Cooper, Don and Maddy Binsted, Joe and Ruth Hawkey, Bill and

Olive Stewart, Brenda Skyrme, Barbara Baggaley, Bruce and Janet Edwards, Frank and Kathleen Hopkinson, George and Rosalie Dixon, Donald and Dorothy Wood, Clifford Ward, Dorothy Kendrick, Angela Weir and Harry Bruce on the team, to name but a few of the many, life at Ellel Grange was definitely not going to be boring - as was always abundantly evident at the annual Christmas party. Watching Grace and the others let their hair down will always be unforgettable!

It was envisaged that the Associate Counsellors would form the backbone of the ministry team on the Healing Retreats as well as share in personal counselling appointments from time to time. In the event they certainly did this, but they did so much more as well, supporting everyone from the Leadership to the YIPs through the ups and downs of a roller coaster ride with God. Peter, and other members of the Leadership, owe much to the Associates personally, as well as on behalf of the whole ministry. They have been a rock solid anchor on which God could depend.

The initial group of Associates almost selected themselves, but many more were needed. A number of people who were then unknown to the pioneer leaders had written offering themselves to the ministry. All who had expressed any interest were invited to a special training and selection weekend at Ellel Grange in February 1987.

First there was teaching about different aspects of healing and information about what the work of an Associate Counsellor was envisioned to be. The leaders tried to get to know as many of the people as possible, and then began to pick out potential Counsellors. All this was important, but God had his hand in the selection procedure as well, in a way that could not have been planned by man.

For reasons Peter could not have understood at the time, God had clearly led him to prepare some teaching for the weekend from the Book of Nahum - not the most well known treatise on the healing ministry! As he studied the book, however, key lessons it contains about spiritual warfare became increasingly obvious. But when should he use this material? It was only as he went down the Ellel staircase to the meeting room for the Sunday morning service that he realised now was the time to speak from the book of Nahum. Instead of teaching anything about counselling or healing, therefore, Peter shared what God had put on his heart from Nahum.

What followed proved to be an unforgettable experience for those present. It seemed something like the day of Pentecost must have been. It was a Baptism, both of fire and of Spirit, for the ministry. Within a few minutes of Peter completing his teaching, the Spirit of God fell in a way that few present had ever seen before. God was cleansing and preparing his people for the task that lay ahead.

For many it was a time of deep repentance as they were putting their lives right with God. For others it was a time of healing and deliverance. For some it was a time of deep intimacy with the Lord when He called them into the ministry. So many people were overcome by an incredible awareness of God that it was impossible to minister to everyone who was in need. No-one who lived through the experience could doubt the reality of God's presence. Nor could they question the fact that God had put His seal on the ministry and upon those He was going to use in its foundation. God's fire was cleansing His people from the inside out.

The Sunday morning service continued throughout the day and long into Monday morning. Edwin Bibby, one of the pioneer Associate Counsellors took a few people aside at about four o'clock in the afternoon to intercede on behalf of those who were in need of healing or deliverance and those who were ministering to them. But the spirit of God fell so heavily on the prayer meeting that they were quite unable to pray in any other way than to cry out to God from the floor - often in tongues, and certainly as Paul described in Romans 8:26, with *"the Spirit himself interceding for us with groans that words cannot express."*

There was hardly anyone in the building, irrespective of whether or not they were actually in the meeting room, who was not deeply affected by what was happening. This extraordinary anointing was heavy on the building and the ministry for several days. People who came to Ellel Grange on the succeeding days were aware that something significant had happened.

Whilst most were blessed by the experience, there were some who felt that being an Associate Counsellor with Ellel Ministries might not be for them after all! But there were others for whom it was the beginning of a decade or more of service in the Kingdom. God used that weekend to call a number of key workers into the ministry whom He used extensively, often in very remarkable ways, in the months and years that were to lie ahead.

Never again has there been a time in the ministry quite like it. It was as if God himself came down and said, *"This is my work, it is not the work of man. I will choose those who will work here and I will have my way in this place."* Whatever interpretation one might put on it, there is no doubt that those whom God encouraged over that weekend to join the team of Associate Counsellors proved to be an extraordinarily faithful and resilient team of men and women who stuck together in the work through many trials and tests that were to follow in the years ahead.

Some of those early Associate Counsellors were to minister on well over a hundred healing retreats as the years went by. They also came to the Grange on the middle nights of dozens and dozens of Training Courses to minister to those who were ready to apply the truths they had been learning on the courses.

Quite a number of people who came into the work as Associate Counsellors then became Associate Teachers and some, even full-time members of the team. At Ellel Grange Barbara Baggaley and Brenda Skyrme have taught on many Training Courses and been leaders on the 9-week schools at Glyndley Manor. At Glyndley Manor, former 9-week School student and Baptist minister, John Glover, is rolling back the years - both as an Associate Counsellor and as a Teacher on Healing Retreats.

At Pierrepont Fred Elgar started his association with Ellel Ministries as an Associate Counsellor at the age of 74. He then became an Associate Teacher, teaching on the Healing Retreats. At the last count he had become a full-time member of the staff as Jill Southern's Deputy Director. His wife Barbara looks after the Pierrepont Bookshop. Fred has a lifetime of ministries behind him, ranging from his years as an Anglican priest to being a Board member of both *Wholeness Through Christ* and *Youth With a Mission.* Now 78, he is not exactly the youngest member of the team, but he makes many people much younger than him feel old!

Whilst it is always good when younger people do become Associate Counsellors, reality states that older people, whose children are grown up, and especially those who are newly retired, are more likely to have the time available to devote to the ministry. Also, it is people from this age group who often have enough experience of life's problems to be very effective helpers of those who are struggling with issues which younger counsellors might not have the maturity to handle. God is a wonderful economist and there is nothing in our past that he is not able to use. Conversely the team have often been surprised at how effective younger members of the team can be. It's as if, in these situations, God gives them His maturity!

It should also be remembered, however, that youthfulness is not just a function of physical age but also of attitude of heart! The young in heart really can be used by God to move mountains and those who wait on the Lord (Isaiah 40:31) really are able to renew their strength, to rise up as if on the wings of an eagle, to run and not be weary, and to walk and not faint. The team of Associate Counsellors are a living demonstration of the truth of this Scripture.

Ellel Grange, Glyndley Manor, Ellel Pierrepont, Ellel Canada, and Ellel East all have a significant team of Associate Counsellors. Without them the work could not function. With them God has performed miracles!

CHAPTER 9

Growth and Development
of Ellel Grange

Early Days at the Grange

Ellel Grange will always be the place where God initiated the ministry, but as other centres have been added to the work its role within the ministry has had to expand and develop. It is now, therefore, not only the Ellel centre for North West England, fulfilling its original vision and purpose, but also the administrative centre of what is rapidly becoming an international ministry, servicing three English centres, two overseas ones and with strong developing links with supporting groups in a number of different countries.

It is important to note that the buildings owned by the ministry are not idols, but were given by God as an essential means of facilitating the vision. Many people who visit a centre talk about it feeling 'so peaceful there', or 'so much at home' or 'so loved and cared for'. We know this is God's heart being expressed and so the buildings themselves play an important part in the healing process, just as other facilities do, such as cars, vans, cookers, tape desks, etc, etc.

During the first full year of the ministry, 1987, there were 19 Healing Retreats, 12 Training Courses and 5 Church visits. Peter was the Director of the ministry and a non-executive Advisory Board had a major role to play in advising and directing the team. Gradually, as the pioneer team grew in experience and numbers, the more senior members evolved into a leadership team. This team met every Monday morning to pray, talk about and plan the ongoing ministry. Major plans were referred to the Advisory Board for either approval or modification.

At one of the Leadership Meetings the team were given a very vivid prophetic picture of the whole work being rather like an old-fashioned sailing vessel. The ship was preparing for a long voyage and there was a sign by the gang-plank against the vessel. It read *"Crew Only - No passengers on this vessel"*. On a sailing ship every member of the crew really matters. If any one member of the crew fails to fulfil their function properly, then the other members of the crew suffer and the progress of the vessel is impeded.

That is a very accurate picture of team ministry in the Body of Christ. Ever since then, on the wall above Peter's desk, there has been a drawing of Scott's vessel *Discovery,* in full sail, leaving Dundee harbour for the Antarctic. It is a constant reminder to him of the calling of God on the ministry and that every single member of the team matters.

On the 30th and 31st October 1987 the first anniversary of purchasing Ellel Grange was celebrated at Lancaster University with a regional teaching conference entitled *Distributing the Power.* Many people were deeply touched by God at the conference, including one lady who had been struggling with what was wrong with her on the inside. She had come to the Lord at the first Vineyard Conference in Lancaster two years previously. She experienced severe manifestations, but her Church were not equipped to cope with her need for deliverance.

At the end of the conference she went back to Ellel Grange. It was the beginning of a dynamic pilgrimage with God as the team ministered to her, on and off, for nearly a year. It was a long and arduous period, both for her and the ministry, but at the end of the time she knew, beyond any shadow of doubt, that Jesus had set her free and that now she could begin to live for Christ, without the many bondages that were holding her to the past. God had worked a miracle in her life.

This was a lonely time for the team as they tried to maintain a balance between inner healing, physical healing and deliverance whilst sticking steadfastly to God's learning curve, as He showed them in person after person what were the roots of their problems. Many of the paths they had to walk seemed like uncharted territory, although they now know that at the same time, in different parts of the world, God was leading others along similar paths.

In every Christian walk there are tests, trials and temptations. Satan, Scripture says, is *"like a roaring lion, seeking whom he may devour"* (1 Peter 5:8). He will always try and push people into making mistakes but each of us has to be personally accountable for the mistakes we make. But if our hearts are right towards God, He will always show where things have gone wrong so that we can get back on track. The team did make mistakes, but they pressed on, determined not to be diverted by the enemy from their vision and calling.

During this period there were a few people who had formerly supported the vision for a healing centre in the North West, but for whom the reality of that vision including deliverance was more than they could embrace.

There were a total of three anniversary conferences (at the 1st, 2nd and 4th anniversaries) at Lancaster University. The second and third conferences, called *Commissioned to Serve* and *See His Glory* respectively, provided an important opportunity for the Ellel teachers to grow in experience and confidence. Marilyn Baker's singing marked out *See His Glory* as being of particular significance.

From Redwards to Kings Lee

The only building on the main Ellel estate that had not been purchased by The Christian Trust, at the time Ellel Grange was acquired, was called *Redwards. Redwards,* a modest, but substantial house on the east side of the property had been sold off by the former owners to help with the major financial costs of the restoration of the Grange. It was being run as an old people's home. As the work expanded it was clear that this property would eventually be needed in the ministry and after long, protracted and somewhat difficult negotiations, arrangements were made with the owners to buy the property and business as a going concern.

Ken Hepworth was a Pastor from East Lancashire. He had been travelling up to Ellel Grange at regular intervals to learn more about the practice of the healing ministry. Ken had, by then, taught on one or two healing retreats and the ministry team were appreciative of his teaching gifts. It became clear that God was calling him into the work. But what would his wife do? As Jean was at that time managing an old people's home, her immediate role in the ministry became obvious! Redwards and its elderly residents became her responsibility.

Redwards was re-named *King's Lee* (meaning *"in the shelter of the King")* - a very suitable name for the care of those in need. With the increasing impact of government and local authority regulations, however, it became clear that the costs of equipping and maintaining the home to modern standards would far outweigh the potential income from the business. Within two years King's Lee was closed down and the remaining elderly residents were found suitable accommodation in other homes nearby - not before, however, at least one of them had found faith in Christ! Very shortly after that Ken and Jean moved to Glyndley

Manor for Ken to fill the teaching vacancy on the team created by Joe and Ruth Hawkey's move to Canada.

At about this time the team were developing a ministry to those with special needs and the availability of a permanent ministry suite had become essential. The upstairs of King's Lee was, therefore, converted to provide this vital facility. The suite contains a bedroom for a counsellee and carer, a lounge, kitchen, bathroom and a small single room for the member of the ministry team on residential duty. It has been in virtually continuous use ever since.

The lower part of King's Lee now houses the service departments which support the wider work of Ellel Ministries at all five centres - publicity, personnel, accounts, secretarial etc. Here, also, is coordinated the extension and development of the work of Church visits, teaching conferences and overseas visits.

The Team Expands

Barry and Jan Jay joined the team at Ellel Grange, as its first Wardens, in January 1987. Their experience in Christian Hotel management, and their loving caring hearts, meant that they were able to establish very high standards for the welcoming side of the ministry right from the earliest days. They were a real gift from God. They were also very special to all the YIPS - many of whom are still in touch with them.

When they joined the team they brought with them Barry's elderly Dad who, though beginning to go senile, especially enjoyed singing the old hymns he had learned in childhood. He never forgot them. They also brought their daughter Sarah, a hairdresser, who, for a couple of years used the hairdressing salon we had inherited from the Health Hydro as her place of work. It was very convenient for the team to have such a facility on the premises, though not particularly attractive financially for Sarah!

The patterns Barry and Jan established for the ministry are still in place today. They laid a practical and godly foundation. After three years of virtually continuous work Barry and Jan took some time out of the ministry before returning, as mentioned elsewhere, to work with Glyndley Manor and, as Ellel Ambassadors, in the development of Prayer Support Groups and manning the stands at conferences and exhibitions.

The first ministry team coordinator at Ellel Grange was Fiona (see also page 159). Ever since she was a teenager God had been using her to get alongside people in need. And pastoral visitation work in her local Church made her very aware that the real needs people had could not easily be met by attending Church services.

In her present teaching ministry she often relates how God showed her, during the early days at Ellel Grange, His heart for the hurting and broken:

> "It was a very wet and windy day. As I hurried the dog along for a necessary walk in the grounds of Ellel Grange, my eyes fixed on a small grey bundle left alone in the adjoining field. I scrambled over two fences, picked up the tiny bundle and placed it inside my coat.

> "There was a faint bleat from a very cold and wet lamb. I made straight for Alec Sayer's farmhouse. He held out his rugged hands and gently held the lamb. 'Don't worry', he said. 'We'll give him a bottle and keep him warm by the fire. He'll be alright.' I had an overwhelming joy within, at having rescued a dying lamb.

> "But through this God showed me that there were many hundreds of 'human lambs' in great need and with no-one to help them. His pain was tangible to me and I began to weep. I realised the price Jesus paid for us. His love for us is so incredibly deep."

Since then God has used Fiona time and time again to minister to those broken lambs who have come to Ellel for help. She is now pioneering a new development in the ministry using creative arts as an aid to releasing the pain and trauma that is so often locked away inside.

In January 1987 'a wee Scottish lass' was seconded from YWAM in Glasgow for six months experience at Ellel Grange. But Mary Munro's time at the Grange stretched into a major calling and now, as ministry manager, she is an extremely experienced and valued senior team member.

Philip Moore took early retirement from Barclays Bank. For a number of years he did a sterling job as Bursar until the work had grown to such an extent that a more comprehensive finance and accounts office was needed. Now, ten years later, he is the Trust Corporation Secretary and a vital member of the Executive Leadership.

Betty Wright served ten years as both a counsellor and as switchboard telephonist. Many is the person (including other team members) who has given thanks to God for her loving counsel and prayers given over the phone. Mike Gatenby came from North Wales to man the kitchens following Judy Allen's retirement. He and his wife Trish, and many others, are people whose commitment and faithful dedication have been at the heart of what God has done at the Grange.

Anne, a friend of Barry and Jan's, offered to come in on a Monday and bake cakes for the team. How welcome her offer was. The team loved her - as well as her cakes! She baked enough to last a week. This simple act of service, which she faithfully carried out almost every Monday for nearly ten years, typifies the spirit of those whom God sent to be part of the team.

David and Bridget Woodhouse came out of Parish Ministry to join the team. Their extensive experience was greatly appreciated as they were able to concentrate, for a period, on counselling and healing ministry. Subsequently David and Bridget returned to Parish life and have pursued a specialist healing ministry alongside their Church responsibilities.

Gabby Llewellyn joined the team almost from the very beginning. Her vibrant personality, energy and ability to make things happen made her, for a number of years, a vital and much loved member of the Ellel Grange management team. Madeline Richey was also involved in the work for a number of years from the beginning and was especially valued for her commitment to intercession and counselling.

When Barry and Jan left the Grange there was an enormous, seemingly unfillable, hole. But with God all things are possible and some visitors to Ellel told their friends Malcolm and Anna Wood about the vacancy. Malcolm and Anna were in the throes of selling their Christian Hotel in North Wales. Yes, they were interested in the job and yes, they would come for an interview.

The Leadership knew immediately that this was the couple. Before long Malcolm and Anna, with their three boys Ian, Andy and Tim were installed in Rose Cottage, adjacent to Ellel Grange. The whole family fitted like a hand in a glove. Malcolm and Anna were ideal for the job. Now seven years later it is hard to imagine Ellel Grange without them.

They now live off base in their own home and Malcolm is responsible for the Site and all the Facilities, and Anna is the Deputy Director of Ellel Grange and the Personnel Director for the whole ministry. Ian found a wife among one of the young people who helped at a holiday school and Ian's wife's parents are now on the team at Pierrepont! Tim wishes they still lived at the Grange!

It would be hard not to mention at this point some of the other very dear colleagues such as Ian Coates, Jeff and Margaret Tye, Pam Mills, Jeremy and Lissa Smith, Geoff Jackson, Paul and Liz Griffin, Roger and Cindy Reeve, Anne and Derek Clarke, Caroline Faunce-Brown, Gwen Collins, Whai Aun and Jonathan Cansdale. All of these, and many others, have, through the developing years, given unswerving support to Ellel Ministries and continue to do so.

It is also right to mention just some of those who have received long-term ministry and ongoing help at Ellel Grange - people such as Wendy, Chris and Rachel. These three subsequently became team members. As God brought healing to them, and many others, deep lessons were learned which, at a later date, were used to bless many, many people.

A New Place and a New Name

With the extension of the work to another location, Glyndley Manor, attention had to be given to the overall name of the ministry. It could no longer be referred to simply as Ellel Grange. On investigation the word Ellel was found to be a modern-day corruption of the old English name of the community, meaning *"All Hail"*. In Hebrew the word El represents God and Ellel would mean God of God's or King of Kings and Lord of Lords. In ancient Cantonese a word that sounds like Ellel means *"love flowing outwards"*.

When the various meanings of the word Ellel are run together, they very effectively sum up the whole ministry - *"All hail Jesus, King of Kings and Lord of Lords, love flowing outwards"*. It would be hard to improve on this as a descriptive name so it was decided, therefore, to adopt universally the name Ellel Ministries for the future work.

Expanding Horizons and Changing Leadership

As the work grew beyond Ellel Grange and Glyndley Manor into Eastern Europe and Canada, the time Peter was able to spend at Ellel Grange was getting less and less. A new Leader of the work at the Grange was essential. The first person to step into the role was Steve Hepden. Before joining the work Steve, and his wife Chris, had extensive leadership experience with Bristol Christian Fellowship. Steve had also developed a teaching speciality in the area of rejection, a problem often leading to major healing needs.

During their three and a half years with the ministry Steve taught extensively at the various centres and served as Director of Ellel Grange and as part of the Leadership Team. He and Chris left the work in 1996 to develop their own itinerant ministry under the name Philos Trust. Steve and Chris's ministry was much appreciated and valued. They became great encouragers and provided much inspiration to the team.

Clive Corfield was another gifted teacher who served the Lord within the work at Ellel Grange for a limited season. For nearly three years he taught very effectively on a series of different training courses and conferences and also on the 9-week Schools. At the end of 1996 Clive revived a ministry name he and his wife Karen had used in earlier years, and re-established themselves independently as Sovereign Ministries.

Jim and Muriel Russell, friends of Malcolm and Anna visited the Grange from time to time. They were always challenged by what they saw. Jim later took early retirement from his work with Eagle Star Insurance and joined the team. Jim's gentle teaching gift gradually emerged, a gift that was especially appropriate for the hurting people who come on Healing Retreats. Muriel's natural warmth in welcoming people endeared her to many visitors to the

Grange. And as 'Aunty Muriel' on the holiday schools children loved her.

Jim then stepped into the role of Director of Ellel Grange and for three years he and Muriel held the work on course, teaching many Healing Retreats and Training Courses. He always referred to himself, however, as a reluctant leader and it was no surprise, therefore, when he and Muriel retired for a second time!

And so the scene was set for Ken and Jean Hepworth's return from Ellel Canada to Ellel Grange - the place where, ten years earlier, he had come as a young Pastor to gain experience of the healing ministry! Ken took up his appointment as Centre Director in September 1997 with Anna Wood as his Deputy Director.

The work of leading an Ellel Centre carries with it considerable responsibility. It is not an easy load to carry with pressures being experienced from both the ministry itself and the consequences of the impact of the work on personal living. It is like living Church life, family life and work life seven days a week with the same people every day! Even though regular periods of time off are possible for most people, there are many 'odd' hours that have to be worked, issues to handle and programmes to fulfil.

It can be likened to running a ship, with a crew that have to meet the requirements of many different programmes and schedules at the same time as keeping the sails trimmed and the vessel on course! It is not surprising that, for some, a short season of this type of work, followed by a period without such responsibility, is needed. God has clearly shown that there will be some who work in this way for a season. Then they may move on to something completely different, sometimes with a period of part-time involvement. We see this as a positive way of helping some people to prepare for new roles in other spheres of God's calling.

It is not only leaders of the work who feel the pressure. Working in the ministry can be like living in a spiritual, emotional and physical 'greenhouse'. The very factors which attract people to come and work in an atmosphere of spiritual reality are, for some, more than they can stand for long. Inevitably, therefore, as in any good garden, pruning is occasionally necessary - especially where there has been the pressure associated with quick growth.

The process of pruning, however, can itself be painful. It is not easy when people leave the work, for whatever reason. But God has clearly been in the process and the Leaders have had to stand by and watch, almost helplessly, as God has shaken and pruned the ministry. At times they have wondered when, or even if, it would stop, but a deep sense of peace has prevailed as they realised if God was doing it, then the end-result could only strengthen the work.

As a result the team has emerged immensely encouraged knowing that Ellel Ministries was conceived in the heart of God, the work is His and His alone, and that it must remain in that place of security with Him. Otherwise, no-one on the team could have survived the fire and the testing which they have had to go through, or the cleansing and purging that has taken place. They have had to find God, and hang on to Him in circumstances which have sharpened and developed their Christian character.

In every way it has been a daily walk of faith and obedience - perhaps the two most important keys for remaining under the anointing of the Holy Spirit? It has brought challenges from without and within. At times it has seemed as though every power of darkness has been unleashed against the ministry. But in the midst of all this the most precious place has been before God in prayer, allowing him to fashion human vessels for His glory. The power of prayer has been central. God has been especially teaching the team about His heart for Godly order in the lives of both His children and the Church. In a very real way healing is simply the restoration of Godly order in every area of a person's life.

The management and leadership of the work is currently in greater unity and is stronger and more secure. But what God has done in bringing the team to this place can only be for a purpose - that the ministry will move forward into a period of greater effectiveness and fruitfulness. *"My Father's glory"*, Jesus said, *"is shown by you bearing much fruit."* (John15:8) The prayer of the team is that as the world experiences times of great spiritual darkness, the ministry will increasingly become effective as a place of hope and healing for those in need, and a beacon of light and truth in the Body of Christ.

On several occasions there here have been requests to the Ellel team to start a Church so that people could come to worship at at the Grange, or one of the other centres, every week. The Leadership have never believed, however, that this is what God was calling them to do. The calling on the ministry is to be a servant to the Body of Christ and for team members to be part of the local Church.

The Chapel

The only building at Ellel Grange which remains undeveloped and unused is the Chapel. The Chapel was built in 1873 as a place of Anglican worship for the estate workers.

The Chapel is a fine architectural structure, having one of the only two octagonal stone spires in the country. It fell into disuse, however, after the war, when the number of estate workers was reduced to an absolute minimum. The last service took place there in 1946. The previous owners of Ellel Grange were, sadly, responsible for stripping and selling the contents, furnishings and windows of the chapel so that it is now nothing more than a derelict shell.

The Leadership Team do, however, have a vision for the chapel. They want to see it restored as a ministry centre so that they can minister into deep broken-ness and re-build peoples' lives without the noise and bustle of the conference activity in Ellel Grange itself. Planning permission will not be a problem, provided the design does not interfere with the external outline of the building, which is protected by its designation as a Listed Building. All that stands in the way of the old Church being restored to dynamic life is the money to do the job.

Malcolm and his Site and Facilities team are ready to spring into action the moment funds are available. In faith this project is moving ahead slowly. Electricity was installed in the summer of 1998 as the first step in believing for its eventual restoration. One function of the restored chapel will be to house facilities for healing through creative arts. Much blessing has already been experienced by those going through in-depth ministries as God uses their natural creativity to bring hope and restoration to broken lives.

There is so much to thank God for in the history and development of Ellel Grange. It has become a haven for the hurting and a place of training for their shepherds. It will continue to fulfil the vision for which it was first acquired for many years to come.

CHAPTER 10

"The Battle" in Budapest

and other events in Eastern Europe

In 1989, when the first Conference at Brighton was all over, the team retreated to their hotel for a time of thanksgiving and communion. Just as this special service was concluding, Bill Subritzky turned to Peter and said, *"I believe the Lord is telling me that this team is going to be strategic in Eastern Europe and Russia."* This was to prove to be a very accurate prophetic word.

The team placed Bill's word alongside other things to test and pray about that the Lord had already been showing to the leadership. They knew that if this word really was of God, He would open the doors for its fulfilment at the right time. Three months later Peter was invited to take part in a mission to Romania, just after the revolution had brought a measure of liberty to the people.

A Swedish evangelist had been blessed by the Lord at Brighton and felt led to ask Peter and others if they wanted to go with him. Joe Hawkey, one of the Ellel Grange Associate Counsellors, was one of those who also went with Peter. The journey was to take them through Budapest, the capital of Hungary.

One of the foreign guests at Brighton had been Zoltan Szocs. God touched him deeply at the conference and healed something in his life that had been a prevailing condition for fourteen years. He lived in Budapest and worked at the University. On their way back from Romania Joe and Peter met up with Zoltan in the Aero Hotel. It was to be one of those divine appointments through which God would show something of how He was going to use Ellel Ministries in Eastern Europe.

Zoltan shared with Peter and Joe how his late father had prayed for years for a centre in Hungary to which Pastors could go for rest, recuperation and training. In the communist era the oppression they were under was heavy and constant. When his father died Zoltan carried on the intercession for his father's vision to be fulfilled.

As Joe, Zoltan and Peter shared and prayed, they sensed that God was drawing aspects of the two visions together and that the time was now right for both Ellel Ministries to begin a work in Eastern Europe and to look to God for the fulfilment of Zoltan's father's vision. As a first step they began to think in terms of bringing *The Battle Belongs to the Lord* to Budapest.

At that time, the Soviet Communists were still in power, but their days in Hungary were definitely numbered. There were days of opportunity ahead. But who would go to Hungary and pioneer the work?

By this time Otto and Sharon Bixler had uprooted themselves from California and were just settling into their new roles at Ellel Grange. Otto went with Peter and Joe on a further exploratory visit to Budapest. Something of what God was doing in Eastern Europe began to touch Otto's pioneer spirit, perhaps through his European ancestry. The seeds of his future ministry were beginning to germinate as his heart was opened to the needs of those wonderful Eastern European people.

The First Hungarian Conference

Before long Otto was back in Hungary again, this time with Sharon. They threw themselves into building relationships with the Hungarians and planning to bring *The Battle Belongs to the Lord* to Budapest in 1991. Back in England plans were already well advanced for running *The*

Battle Belongs to the Lord again at Brighton the following year. The teaching team, including Bill Subritzky, were all willing to do the conference twice. Once in Brighton and then again the week after in Budapest.

The former Communist Party Conference Hall was booked for the occasion. Having been fitted with multilingual facilities and ear phones in every seat, it was ideal for the event. Otto and Sharon began to train local individuals to help with the conference. Some sixty Associate Counsellors largely from the UK, but including a team from Canada, agreed to come and form the experienced nucleus of the ministry team.

Information about the conference went out all over Eastern Europe. In the event there were delegates from thirteen different nations represented and translation facilities were provided from the platform for English and Hungarian (via interpretation) and a further six languages were catered for via ear-phones from the translation booths which had been installed to aid communication between Communist Party delegates from various nations in the former Soviet Bloc.

It was to be a truly international event, but for most languages there were not as yet any interpreters. As delegates arrived they were asked *"Do you speak English?"* by one of the British team. If they could understand and answer that question in the positive there was a possibility that they may be able to translate the teaching into their own language. Interpreters were found for Polish, Romanian, Russian, Czeck, Bulgarian and German.

The main Russian interpreter was Valery Solin. Valery formerly worked for the Russian authorities. He was converted following a vision God gave him of a man dying on a cross. He found a confiscated Bible and read about Jesus. This led to his conversion, following which he joined a Pentecostal Church.

One day, because he had a smattering of English through listening to English language pop music on the radio, he was asked if he would translate the message of a visiting preacher who had no interpreter. Valery protested his inability, but because there was no-one else who knew anything in English, he stood up to try and interpret. It was, for him, an impossible situation - until, that is, God gave him the gift of tongues - in English! He then learnt to write the language and began to translate Christian books into Russian - including Peter's books on *Healing Through Deliverance*. He now runs a 'translation factory', translating, printing and distributing as many different Christian books as donated funds will allow. The books are then distributed at nominal cost to pastors all over Russia and the former Russian States.

Valery had come to Budapest for the conference with a few friends by train from Estonia. They had been able to buy their tickets in Russia, but because of exchange restrictions were not allowed to bring any more than a few valueless roubles out of the country to live on. Only later was the story told of how they would have been destitute in Budapest, without food or lodging, were it not for Valery's amazing gift of faith to be able to trust his Heavenly Father for providing all his needs. He had really come to know God as Jehovah Jireh - God my provider.

As they walked along the pavement in Budapest, after the first evening's meeting, Valery kicked against a packet of something on the floor. In the dark, he bent down to pick it up. It was a rolled-up bundle of Hungarian bank notes. They were secured by a rubber band and there was no name, address or any possible means of identifying their source. Valery knew this was God's provision. God had provided enough for him and his Estonian friends to live comfortably in Budapest during the conference and be able to return home safely when it was all over. There are many occasions on which God has met Valery's needs in supernatural ways such as this.

One man at the conference had been prayed for well in advance of the event by a member of the English ministry team. Twenty five years earlier Hazel Gifford's heart had been stirred by reading about the plight of believers in Eastern Europe. In a dream God showed her a man in prison. He was unforgettable - thin, poorly clad, with damaged and broken teeth and the marks of hardship and suffering clearly upon him. She knew she had to pray for him and did so consistently for many months, never knowing whether he was a specific individual or a representative of a group of people.

Hazel writes, "Imagine my amazement when, twenty five to thirty years later, at the Budapest Conference, I looked up whilst serving lunches to delegates to see the man of my dream. It was impossible to speak to him then; I just prayed that if it were right the Lord would make the opportunity. Later that day, as I sought out a newly appointed ministry place in the balcony, I was joined by a group of Romanians, and my friend was among them. Miraculously an interpreter was to hand.

"He had been a Christian for only eight years but had since suffered for his faith, having to live sometimes with the animals. He had been in prison years earlier but not for his faith, for other things. When he realised that God so loved and cared for him that He'd laid him on another's heart, hundreds of miles away all those years ago, he was overwhelmed and became deeply grateful to God.

"The hugs and tears spoke volumes, overcoming the language barrier, and I will never forget the sight of him praising God, with tears streaming down his face. He had cycled many miles to the Romanian border to get to the conference. The train fare paid by others was out of the question for him, being equivalent to two months wages."

While this conference was taking place the local papers carried the celebratory news that the last Russian Commanding Officer had finally left Hungary. While the team were teaching about freedom in Christ, the Hungarian people regained their freedom from oppression. In Hungary the success and fruit of the conference opened the door for Ellel to begin pioneering trips from Budapest into the surrounding nations.

The Work in Eastern Europe Develops

The main translator into Hungarian for the second time of running *The Battle Belongs to the Lord* in Budapest was Zsolt Simonfalvi, an outstanding young Pastor whom everyone recognised as having an important teaching gift of his own. His contribution to Ellel's work in Eastern Europe was significant. It was his words that introduced much of the teaching and ministry to the Hungarian people. Tragically Zsolt later contracted leukemia and even though the whole team prayed their heart out for him, his wife Aniko and their two children, Zsolt went to be with the Lord.

Other conferences in Hungary were to follow *The Battle*. In 1992 the conference was called *The Anointing of God*. Again there were many delegates who travelled from the surrounding nations. And this time, immediately after the Hungarian Conference was over, the teaching and ministry team broke up into four separate units. Three units travelled to the Ukraine, Lithuania and Estonia and a fourth remained to minister in a local Church in Hungary. These visits taught the team much about both the conditions the people had endured under communist domination and the amazing courage of the Christians who had stood firm and remained faithful to God in extreme and testing circumstances.

By now Otto and Sharon were well-established and God was using them to build bridges within Hungary as well as to Christian groups in the surrounding nations. They made several trips to the Ukraine, usually in distinctly inhospitable, freezing conditions, to people who had no heating and little to eat. But the people's hearts were always very warm and full of generosity. They were hungry for scripturally based teaching which would enable them to minister healing and hope to their own people.

A teaching conference followed in the former closed secret city of Svedlobost. During one of the preliminary training days a man was heard to mutter, *"It's worth it. It's worth it."* Eventually he explained what he meant. He was a Pastor and in order to pay the rail-fare to come to the training day he had sold his family's only means of support - the family cow. When he heard and understood the teaching, for him it was worth it. The lessons he was learning were of more worth to him than the family cow!

Few people in the West can understand the spiritual and physical deprivations that our brothers and sisters in these former communist states have had to endure, and the sacrifices they willingly make on behalf of God's people. The team have been greatly privileged to be able to stand with them, learn from them and bring the healing love of Jesus into their lives.

One nation that was well-represented at the Budapest conferences was Poland. Even before the conferences God had been working in the lives of Pastor Bolek Paliwoda and his wife Eva, preparing them for a significant role amongst the Polish people of all denominations.

At Budapest, Bolek knew that the teaching he heard was what his own people needed to hear. A series of teaching conferences followed in Wroclaw and several of his people came on the 9-week School at Glyndley Manor. Bolek is now heading up a small but developing Ellel work in Poland and has already begun to fulfil an important teaching role.

In 1997 the Conference in Kremenchug (Ukraine) broke new ground for Ellel Ministries in a very important way. It was the first conference at which the teaching team included Eastern European leaders. Bolek was one of those teachers. He spoke in Polish and was translated into Russian. For Otto and Sharon this was a highly significant moment as they saw local people, whom they had nurtured and trained, carrying forward the teaching that Ellel had first taught at *The Battle Belongs to the Lord* in Budapest.

Two other Eastern European speakers at Kremenchug were Laci and Ibolya Mezes. Laci is pastor of a well-known Church in Budapest and now has many stories of his own to tell which confirm the fruit of the teaching. His wife is a medical consultant. She went to the Budapest conference admitting to a touch of scepticism, but also with a willingness to be convinced by God that healing and deliverance were for today and were real.

Not only was she convinced by what she saw God do at the conference, but she started to apply the teaching herself and began to see God bring remarkable healing and deliverance to some of her patients and members of the Church for whom she was praying - including those who had been chronically ill with asthma for many years.

Ibolya has a well-developed sense of humour and the way she tells the stories of what God has done brings tears of laughter and joy to the eyes. She and Laci both taught in Kremenchug. Not only did they teach in 1997, but their hearts were moved to commit themselves to return to the Ukraine on a later occasion with members of their Church. This they did in June 1998.

In 1993 a large teaching and ministry team went to St. Petersburg. Russians at the earlier conference had been wanting to see *The Battle Belongs to the Lord* brought to their own nation. Valery Solin provided much spiritual encouragement and muscle and eventually the conference banner was raised for the first time on Russian soil. Many obstacles had to be overcome as Otto and Valery pressed on through the difficulties to arrange a venue and organise publicity to local Church leaders. The conference broke new ground for both the team and the delegates.

At the end of the conference a man came rushing forward to present the team with a wonderful antique brass samovar as a gift from the delegates - most of whom had contributed a few roubles each to the purchase. This precious token of their love and appreciation was, sadly, stolen from Ellel Grange in 1995 by burglars who will never understand that by stealing property such as this they are robbing God's people of a reminder of His faithfulness. But no burglar can ever rob God of the deposit of faith and hope that was left in the heart of the Russian people.

People who have lived under the communist systems have been under enormous spiritual oppression. At the 1993 Hungarian Conference, immediately prior to St. Petersburg, the Lord had shown Peter how oppression of a spiritual nature can be reflected onto the body. When he asked how many people were afflicted by back problems, at both Budapest and St. Petersburg, the response from the people was overwhelming. It seemed as if as many as 75% of the people were affected. When they forgave their communist oppressors, and received prayer for deliverance, something very powerful was broken over them and there was much healing.

Since then there have been many, many people who have reported being healed of their back conditions. People like Christina* from Kremenchug in the Ukraine. At the Kremenchug conference she was in severe pain because of a spinal condition that was getting progressively more twisted and painful as she grew older. When she forgave the communists she felt something happen inside her, and when Peter prayed for deliverance from the platform she was immediately and totally healed.

She danced for joy on the platform at what God had done. Four months later God provided the money for her to go to the 9-week School at Glyndley Manor. Her only desire was to get trained, so that she could go back home and bless her own people with what God had already blessed her.

While Christina was being prayed for on the platform a man in the balcony recognised the ministry need in his wife. She had been facially deformed since being damaged at birth. The man ministered to his wife by copying what Peter was doing on the platform. At one stage everyone heard the cry of a *"baby"* as all the pain and trauma she had experienced at birth was released and healed by God. Later she came running down to the platform showing everyone how her face had been healed also. She had experienced a miracle of God's healing love.

Whilst there has already been an enormous amount of blessing in Russia and Eastern Europe, the work there is still in its infancy. Otto, Sharon and the small team are having to spread themselves very thinly over a vast terrain. They are praying hard for more workers who are willing to lay down their lives in Eastern Europe and the former Russian states to be added to the team. They are praying, too, that the next major landmark in the training of more leaders will soon be achieved - the opening of the first Ellel Ministries Russian Language Training School, probably in 1999.

CHAPTER II

Ur Retje

The Lord God's Meadow

Conferences in Lithuania, Estonia, Poland, Ukraine, Hungary and Russia have all played a significant part in training and equipping leaders in Eastern Europe. But the task is vast and limitations on staff and money make it impossible to tirelessly travel and teach over the vast terrains involved. After the walls of oppression came down there was an explosion of new Churches. Many of them are led by young men and women in their early twenties. They have had no training and are desperately in need of discipling and teaching.

For all but a very small handful the costs of getting to the west for training are prohibitive. Unless they can find sponsorship and understand and speak English well, training at a UK school is out of the question. But getting to Hungary is within the realms of possibility, and with the vision for putting on training schools in Russian and other Eastern European languages, the language barrier can be overcome.

Part of the vision that God gave to Ellel for Eastern Europe was the establishment of a training base in Hungary. Leaders could then come from all over Eastern Europe and Russia to be trained at a place they could afford to reach.

In the old days of the USSR, the Soviet authorities insisted that, irrespective of their national language, all citizens of member states had to learn Russian. As a result of this imposition, which most non-Russians hated and resented, Russian has become the common language of communication in that part of the world, in much the same way as English has become the common language of communication in much of the rest of the world. This means that Russian can be used as the primary language of teaching for people from many different nations. What the Soviets imposed for their political purposes can now be used by God for His!

An Ellel Centre in Hungary

Even on their first visit to Hungary the team were praying about the location of an Ellel Ministries centre. It was during the second conference in Budapest that a small group drove all over the region looking at old buildings which could be converted into a teaching and ministry centre. The condition of those available, however, was always so derelict that the costs of restoration would far outweigh their value and usefulness. The thought of building a new centre began to seem very attractive. But where should it be, and would one ever be allowed to buy land in this country where private ownership of land was virtually non-existent?

As Peter studied and prayed over the map around Budapest he was inexplicably drawn to one particular area. He clearly sensed God leading him in this direction. He pointed the hired mini-bus towards the north-west of Budapest to look around. The walls of an estate looked promising, but on investigation they were found to enclose the Hungarian Botanical Gardens. But yes, the curator did speak English and he did know someone (in Orbottyan) who might know somewhere suitable for the work that was described to him.

Next stop was Orbottyan - to meet Peter Fekete. Peter was the Minister of the local Reformed Church and he and his wife were also wardens of a children's home for the mentally handicapped. He could speak no English and his wife could only manage a few words, but in those few minutes of precious fellowship God did a work of bonding which transcended all the barriers of language and culture.

Peter Fekete's wife understood enough of what was being said to get out a map and point out an area of land, of which the Children's Home occupied a small corner. That afternoon, and again the following morning with a larger group of team members, they walked the land. It seemed as though their spirits were singing and God was saying this is the place. It was an extraordinary moment. Sadly, Peter Fekete died before he was able to see these plans come to fruition. But God had used him as a very important bridge for the work of Ellel Ministries into Eastern Europe.

At that time the team had no idea if the land was even for sale. They had no way of investigating its availability. They did not speak the language and the prospects were very much less than encouraging! But if this really was God, then surely He would show them the way? They went back to Budapest and joined with the rest of the Western team for an end of conference thanksgiving meal at a local hotel.

As it happened the team were not the only people using the hotel that night. There was a crowd of somewhat exubriant folk celebrating in fancy dress. *"What are you doing?"*, one of them was asked, as he stood out amongst them resplendent in the upper part of a dinner jacket, balloons and boxer shorts! *"Oh, we are fun runners,"* came the reply. *"We have just run a half-marathon round Budapest and this is our way of winding down."* The man who spoke had an Australian accent.

"And what do you do in Budapest," he was asked. *"I'm in real estate,"* came the reply. *"I help western organisations buy land and property in Hungary. I believe I'm the only*

English speaking land agent in the country right now and I employ a Hungarian surveyor to help me with all the complexities of Hungarian law." His name was Mike Carroll.

Mike had no idea at the time why those who had walked the land at Obottyan that morning were so stunned at what he had just said. For on the very day that God had shown them the land, Peter was introduced to the only English speaking person in the whole of Hungary who could have helped them buy it! Out of thirteen million people in the nation, the very first stranger they were to meet was the one God was going to use.

Ur Retje

But that was not the only miracle associated with this particular piece of land. Why was it that their spirits had so risen with excitement when they went on the land? Why did other discerning people who went on the land subsequently have a similar impression and, even, sense the presence of angels? It was only some three months later that the picture began to unfold.

What they discovered was that this particular piece of land was called, on the land map, *Ur Retje.* That is Hungarian for *"The Lord God's Meadow"!* In 1928 the Professor of Divinity in Budapest had a vision to establish a home to help some widows and orphans from World War 1 whose need was getting desperate. He identified the estate at Orbottyan as being suitable for this work. It consisted of a typical Hungarian country house and about 76 acres of land. It was for sale but he had no money.

The owners did have another buyer, but because they believed in what Professor Kovacs was trying to do they were willing to give him until 3.00pm on March 21st 1928 to find the money. Otherwise it would be sold at that time to the other buyer. Professor Kovacs prayed and shared the vision with others but nothing happened. Even on the morning of the 21st March he had no money and was going to have to let the property go.

Then he got a 'wire' from London. Lord Rothermere, owner of the Daily Mail and a man with a number of other business and personal interests in Hungary, had heard about the project and said that he would fund it. The full purchase price was being wired to his bank in Budapest that very day.

Time was of the essence. Professor Kovacs had to collect the money, organise a lawyer to draw up the contract, make the 25 kilometre journey out of Budapest to Orbotyan and complete the purchase by 3.00pm - otherwise he would lose the estate. He made it by five to three thanks to Lord Rothermere's donation. Lord Rothermere himself went out to Hungary to be present at the dedication of the land.

As a sign of thanksgiving to God the land was not only dedicated to God, but renamed *Ur Retje, The Lord God's Meadow.* And this was the self-same piece of land on which, 63 years later, the Ellel team walked and where God had said they were to build their training and ministry centre. It had already been set apart for the Kingdom so many years ago. The original house had been added to over the years, but only one small area of the land was being used by the Children's Home. Due to the war, and the subsequent communist take-over, only a very small part of the land had yet been used for the purposes of God. It's time had not yet come.

Inside the original house a pair of hands had been carved in stone, in which a child was safely nestled. Against the carving is the Scripture reference Isaiah 49:15-16, which includes those wonderful words, *"See, I have engraved you on the palms of my hands."* These words have often been important within the work of Ellel Ministries when ministering to people who have been very hurt in their childhood.

The battle to acquire the land for Ellel Ministries then began. It is a long story involving many intricacies of Hungarian law and, it seems, determined spiritual opposition. But by a miracle of God's grace all 46 of the inheriting cooperative owners, who were now legally responsible for the land, were happy to sell to Ellel Ministries and two thirds of the land has now been bought. The final third still awaits the resolution of some complex technical legal obstacles with the Hungarian Government.

In order to help with providing up-front capital for the land-purchase a very generous loan was provided by John Horne of Golden Stable Trust which is gradually being paid off with a regular percentage of donation income for the work in Eastern Europe. Without this significant contribution it would not have been possible to move quickly enough so as to secure the land at the critical time when it became available.

Establishing the Base

It was essential that Ellel should establish a permanent presence on the land as soon as possible, but the only original building on the site was a single story, semi-derelict washing and toilet block which had been constructed for use by campers in the summer months. This building was, therefore, designated for eventual occupancy by a Hungarian family, Miki Horvath, his wife Timi and their children, who were to become the first residents as watchmen of Ur Retje. But much had to be done to convert this unlikely building into a family home capable of withstanding the cold Hungarian winters.

At this point John Allen, the Ellel Grange carpenter and builder, came on the scene. He gathered together an emergency flying-squad of four builders and labourers and drove from England with as much equipment and materials as possible to do the job. They bought other materials locally and they were joined on the site by some Hungarian supporters of Ellel Ministries. In an extraordinary period of just over two weeks, they converted the derelict shell into what has been a very successful and attractive family home. No-one now would recognise the humble origins of the property. It was a dynamic example of just what can be done when there is a unity of heart and purpose.

Later, Hungarian building contractors moved in to construct the first major building on the site, which houses the meeting room and administrative offices. This is expected to become usable during the latter half of 1998 when the essential services are laid on to the building. Ellel Ministries are praying that by the end of 1998 they will have received enough donations to equip the administrative building and to build and equip the residential student accommodation, so that they can start Hungarian Healing Retreats and Training Courses, and host the first Russian Language Ellel Ministries Training School, on The Lord God's Meadow in 1999.

Ur Retje will then be fulfilling a purpose far wider in influence than might ever have been envisaged by Professor Kovacs. But in the economy of God the vision of Professor Kovacs, to minister to hurting people, the victims of war, is not very far removed from the vision that God has given to Ellel Ministries to care for the damaged and hurting sheep, the victims of a spiritual war.

It would take a book in itself to tell in detail the amazing story of how the team, and especially Otto and Sharon, battled to acquire for God these 76 acres of beautiful and productive Hungarian land. The financial sacrifices alone of so many people is extremely moving. Only God knows the full extent of His purposes for Ur Retje.

With further signs of persecution of Christians in Russia and the former Russian States, and the possibility of the doors closing once again, we believe God will use the Hungarian nation, and especially Ur Retje to be a safe place for training and help in days of political turmoil. The full story is yet to unfold. Time may pass, people may come and people may go, but in the end nothing can stand in the way of the purposes of God. For Ellel Ministries the words Ur Retje will always be a permanent reminder of God's faithfulness across the generations.

CHAPTER 12

Glyndley Manor

Geoff Shearn's Vision

In October 1986, the same month that the Christian Trust acquired Ellel Grange, another group of Christians bought Glyndley Manor, a country house at the other end of England. Glyndley is an old manor house with a history going back to the days of Elizabeth I and is located in lovely Sussex countryside, near Hailsham, just five miles from the sea at Eastbourne.

Several years earlier Geoff Shearn, well known in the Christian music world through Hosanna Music, had received a vision of a house in the country with little houses in its grounds. He saw people with sad faces going into the big house and then leaving with happy smiling faces. The change on their faces was the consequence of what God did for them inside the building. Geoff began looking for the building, but to no avail and after some years was beginning to give up on the vision.

One day, at a meeting, a complete stranger gave Geoff a specific word of encouragement not to give up on the vision God had given him. The lady knew nothing about his vision, but added that God was going to act on it soon. Shortly after this Geoff discovered that Glyndley Manor, a country hotel not far from his home, was for sale. It was just as God had shown him in the vision some ten years earlier. In the grounds there was an estate of small holiday bungalows exactly like the small houses of his dream. Yet at the time of his vision these had not even been built!

In a very scriptural manner Geoff's family, with three other families who had also adopted the vision as their own, sold everything they had (their homes) in order to acquire *"the field in which the treasure was hidden."* Glyndley Manor, the treasure, was secured for its future use. The four families moved in and lived in the Manor.

There is a video-recording in existence of Geoff Shearn sharing the story of his vision at a meeting in Brighton a year or so after this. The families began to operate the main part of the building as a Christian Hotel. Meanwhile a section of the property was used as offices for Graham Kendrick's music ministry and other Christian enterprises.

After four years the music activities had grown and needed more space. Running a hotel and the enlarged musical activities together became incompatible and the families began to feel the need to look for new premises. Geoff still knew the vision was unfulfilled and struggled within himself until one day he had to admit that it was God's vision not his own personal property. Just then a visitor to Ellel Grange, who supported the ministry, put Geoff Shearn in touch with Peter Horrobin, making a vital link between the original vision and its eventual fulfilment.

For several years many people from the south of England had been praying and pressing Ellel to open a similar centre somewhere in the south of the country. Some of these supporters and Ellel team members visited Glyndley and reported back. Although the building was different from Ellel Grange and had some limitations, the positive reports encouraged the Ellel Leadership to take steps to acquire Glyndley Manor as a base in which the ministry could be replicated in the south of England.

It was easy to see how some strategic alterations could be made to double the floor space of the largest room to provide an excellent meeting room, capable of holding up to

A Centre for Christian Healing, Counselling and Training

Ellel Grange
THE CHRISTIAN TRUST

A PERSONAL WORD FROM THE DIRECTOR

It is my privilege to introduce you to the work of Ellel Grange. Specialising in Christian Counselling and Healing it will be a place of training for those important ministries and a place where personal help will always be available to those in need.

People today are not only in need of physical healing. There are also those who are suffering the consequences of broken homes, child abuse, drug addiction, pornography and the occult — to quote but a few of today's damaging influences.

Their effect can be beyond comprehension to those who are not affected — but for those who are, we believe that the Christian healing ministry is the only long-lasting answer. That is why the establishment and work of Ellel Grange is of such vital importance at the present time.

We are thankful to God for the vision He has given for this work and for the provision of an ideal building in an outstandingly convenient location. For the ministry to become established, however, it will require the determined commitment and generous giving of many people. Will you join those who are already committed to its fulfilment by giving careful consideration to the contents of this brochure.

Peter Horrobin

THE VISION

The vision for a healing and training centre in the North West of England originated about ten years ago. Since then a small group of Christians in the region have been praying and working towards its fulfilment. Now, with wide support from within the region, encouragement from national Christian leaders and with a suitable building in prospect, the vision can be realised.

The healing and counselling ministry that will be conducted at Ellel Grange will be interdenominational in foundation and practice. It will be firmly based on the love of God, the saving and healing power of Jesus Christ, the work of the Holy Spirit and the teaching of Scripture.

The ministry will be conducted by a resident team of people who are experienced in the counselling and healing ministries. They will be assisted by individuals from right across the region who will help to provide the 24-hour ministry cover on a rota basis, and a large team of Associate Counsellors who will share in the ministry from time to time as occasion demands.

The whole ministry will be conducted under the guidance of the Advisory Board and with the encouragement and support of the Council of Reference. The work will be administered by The Christian Trust (Registered Charity No. 279927).

* HEALING AND COUNSELLING
  * TRAINING COURSES
    * RETREATS * CONFERENCES

Centre for Christian Healing, Counselling and Training

Ellel Grange
THE CHRISTIAN TRUST

NEWSLETTER
July–August 1986   Number 1

Interest in Ellel Grange is growing. Every day brings letters of encouragement, donations and requests for information. News of the establishment of this regional centre for Christian healing, counselling and training in the North West of England and attracting media attention. The geographical location of Ellel Grange — between Preston and Lancaster and very close to all the M6 exit is absolutely ideal and many local newspapers and radio programmes have given the project coverage.

The Work Begins

The work of Ellel Grange has already begun — ahead of schedule. All the leaflets that have been distributed across the region have not only had the effect of encouraging supporters but also of more encouraging people to come for help. It has been thrilling to see the work in ministry to God's people already — and see people in their time of need and we give God all the glory.

Revealing His plan and purposes, often at crucial times, and keeping us from making this provision and faithfulness being shown through the sacrificial giving in a people, people who have already been healed through the body of Christ.

Many people are asking for details of the training courses — and not just the people in the North West — from as far as possible, but they are now

... expected to start work until early in the New Year. The Advisory Board has now started to meet regularly and one of the responsibilities we have to prayerfully plan the structure of the ministry at Ellel Grange. At its heart will be a husband and wife team who will be the Wardens. They will live in either some Cottages, one of the three self-contained flats within the Grange itself.

The Advisory Board are looking for a couple who have had some experience of healing and counselling ministries, and are big enough to act as house-parents to the team of young people who will be responsible for much of the domestic work. They will also need to have that essential gift of hospitality so that everyone who comes to Ellel Grange will be made and feel welcome.

Supporting the Wardens is another couple living in the building who will be part of the ministry team. The rest of the team will

Ellel Grange from the South

Centre for Christian Healing, Counselling and Training

Ellel Grange
THE CHRISTIAN TRUST

NEWSLETTER
31st October 1986   Number 4

REJOICE!

'Our God Reigns'

Completion on Schedule

Today, Friday the 31st October 1986, purchase contracts for the acquisition of Ellel Grange, the contents and the Chapel were completed on schedule at the agreed date. We rejoice and give thanks to God for His faithfulness.

The past few weeks have been very thrilling as the gap between the cash in hand and what was still needed steadily closed. Just nine days ago we needed a minimum of £56,000, plus pledges to support the repayments on an additional £35,000 of mortgage borrowing so as to bring the loan potential up to our agreed maximum of £175,000.

... seeing the vision for a regional centre become reality at Ellel Grange, the letters and gifts (many of which have clearly been very sacrificial) have been a tremendous encouragement to us.

Each day as the post has arrived, and telephone calls have come in, we have been able to say with the Psalmist:

"The steadfast love of the Lord never fails. His mercy is forever sure, it is new every morning. Great is your faithfulness O Lord."

It has been a privilege and a very humbling experience to be on the receiving end of so much love and encouragement. To all of you

---

Extracts from the first publicity brochure for Ellel Grange, the first Newsletter and the special thanksgiving edition issued on the day purchase was completed

Peter with Sister Aine

Ellel Grange

Malcolm Colmer - For many years a Trustee & Chairman of the Advisory Board

Fred and Betty Horrobin, Peter's parents, on the steps of Ellel Grange

Ellel Grange in winter dress!

Enjoying a meal in the Dining Room

Alec Sayer helping to clear the Grounds of St Mary's Chapel

Maddy & Don Binsted - former Trustee and members of the Support and Advisory Group

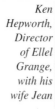

Ken Hepworth, Director of Ellel Grange, with his wife Jean

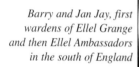
Grace & Bobby Cooper - founder member of Advisory Board

Anna & Malcolm Wood - always at the heart of Ellel Grange

Barry and Jan Jay, first wardens of Ellel Grange and then Ellel Ambassadors in the south of England

Muriel & Jim Russell - former Director of Ellel Grange

Jeremy and Lissa Smith on the Brighton conference stand

John Allen with the Prayer Tower he so lovingly restored

Philip Moore - former Bursar and now Trust Secretary

Barbara Baggaley (top) and Brenda Skyrme (left) - long serving counsellors and Associate Teachers

Bruce and Janet Edwards

The ever popular bookshop

UK Conferences

The Brighton Centre

Bill Subritzky
at "The Battle
Belongs to the
Lord" 1990

Peter teaching
at "The
Church
Ablaze" 1993

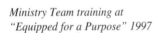

Ministry Team training at
"Equipped for a Purpose" 1997

Communion celebration at "The
Day of His Power" 1995

"The Church Ablaze" Banner, 1993

Guest speakers at Blackpool;
Jackie Pullinger-To (upper)
Chua Wee Hian (lower)

Worship at
"Into all the World", Blackpool 1995

"The Day of His Power" 1995

The Ellel team at "Equipped for a Purpose", 1997

Steve Chua, International worship leader

9-Week School students share testimony at Blackpool

Delegates at "Into all the World"

Tom Marshall - was a frequent visiting teacher and wonderful friend of the ministry

The first edition of "Healing Through Deliverance" (1991) and Ellel publicity

Chris and Jan Mungeam - former Trustees of the ministry and directors of 'Sovereign World', publishers of "Healing Through Deliverance"

Paul & Gretel Haglin, special friends and our advisers in the USA

from left:
Chris Woods, David Noakes and Bishop Graham Dow. Part of the UK Support and Advisory Group

The Ellel team, Christmas 1990

"Ministering to the Sexually Abused" Conference Sheffield 1988

Team visit to the Isle of Wight, 1990

Glyndley Manor

An Eliel Ministries Training Programme

"Jesus called the twelve disciples together and gave them power and authority to drive out all demons and to cure diseases. Then he sent them out to preach the Kingdom of God and to heal the sick." Luke 9:1-2

The International School of Evangelism Healing and Deliverance

held at Glyndley Manor, Sussex, England and now Ellel Canada, Orangeville, Ontario.

Two Schools are held each year in the Spring and the Autumn for a nine week period.

In 1998, the Spring School will take place at Ellel Canada.

Glyndley Manor, Stone Cross, Pevensey, Nr. Eastbourne, East Sussex, BN24 5BS, UK

Commissioning the initial Glyndley Manor leadership team.

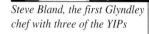
9-Week School with Glyndley team

The welcoming front door

David and Denise Cross, Directors of Glyndley Manor

The bungalows at Glyndley Manor

Steve Bland, the first Glyndley chef with three of the YIPs

Maureen & Pennant Jones - former Director of Glyndley Manor and Trustee

The first Prayer Support Group for Glyndley Manor (1991)

"The Battle" in Budapest 1991

Hungarian pioneers - Sharon & Otto Bixler, Director of Ellel East

Bill Subritzky teaching

Zsolt Simonfalvi translating Peter

Translating the message. One of six booths used at the conference

Ur Retje - Claiming the Land

Establishing the boundaries

God is now fulfilling the vision that Zoltan's father prayed into for 40 years!

"When the work of Ellel Ministries took root in Hungary, it was the fulfilment of a vision given to my Father about 50 years ago!

He wanted to establish a place of refuge and ministry for Christian workers and Pastors. He died before the vision could realise the vision. I inherited the vision and carried it with me through the years. I even tried to realise it, but in vain. When I met with Peter Horrobin in Budapest in 1990 we discovered that the "underlying divine blueprint" was our common call. This is how Ellel Ministries came to life in Hungary."

Zoltan Szoos is Professor of Environmental sciences at the University of Eötvös Loránd and a Trustee of Ellel Ministries in Hungary

"You are to help your brothers . . . until they have taken possession of the land that the Lord your God is giving them . . . " Joshua 1 v13,14

Ellel Ministries Invites You . .

. . to invest in the people of God in Eastern Europe

The full story of how God led us to Ur Retje, this beautiful area of land just north of Budapest, is truly amazing. It began with a prophetic word to the whole team about our ministry in Eastern Europe and Russia. Along the way were training courses and conferences in five Eastern European Countries. And then we found the land! There have been many signs that now is the time and this is the place for a training and ministry centre in Eastern Europe. Your help will bring this vision into reality.

Ur Retje
meaning "The Lord God's Meadow"

Otto with land agent Mike Carroll (1992)

Otto completing the purchase of the first piece of land (1993)

Peter agreeing with the owners for the purchase of the second piece of land

Second base at Veresegyhaz

Training ministry team at our first operational base in Budapest

Ellel East - Establishing the Base

Peter and Otto with the Hungarian Advisors

The redundant toilet block ...

... and after conversion into the Watchman's House (1994)

Zoltan Szocs and Ibolya Mezes at "The Church Ablaze"

Ur Retje - the first dig! 1995

The finished building shell

The basement under construction

Otto at the doors of the new building

The first Prayer Support Group at Ur Retje

Powered up! Our own electricity pylon

The Ellel East Ministry Base from across the lake

Ur Retje - The Lord God's Meadow

Ellel East and Beyond!

"The Battle" in St. Petersburg, Russia (1993)

To Russia with love - the team travel via Aeroflot!

A thanksgiving gift of a Samovar from the Russian people

Karen David in St. Petersburg

Doing business with God

From left: Peter Heywood, Steve Hepden and Clive Corfield on the 1992 Eastern Europe team

Valery Solin, our man in Russia, receiving books for the Russian people from 'Sovereign World Trust'

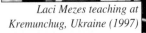

Laci Mezes teaching at Kremunchug, Ukraine (1997)

Bolek and Ewa Paliwoda - leaders of the work in Poland

The joy of healing - Ukrainian style

Peter teaching leaders at the first Polish meeting - translated by Ania (1993)

Ellel Canada

The base in winter, spring and summer

Joe and Ruth Hawkey, first directors of Ellel Canada

Donna Parachin, Director of Ellel Canada

The Ellel Canada Board

Steve Chua (Asst. Director of Ellel Canada) with Donna, Ken Hepworth (previous Director) and Paul and Gretel Haglin

Students on the 9-Week School

THE
**CHURCH
ABLAZE**
CONFERENCE
September 30-13, 1998
Ellel Ministries

THE ELLEL SCHOOL OF
HEALING
Part 1 July 5-17, 1998
Part 2 July 19-31, 1998

Canada's "Battle"! Ken Hepworth teaching (1997)

Into all the World ...

"The Battle Belongs to the Lord", Kuala Lumpar (1994)

Fiona Horrobin with Florence Wang & Linda Tang from Kuala Lumpar

Refreshments at the Sabah conference (1994)

Vincent Lau, Vicar of St. Gabriel's, Kuala Lumpar

Wong Kim Kong who first invited the team to Malaysia (1993)

Singapore prayer supporters

Hong Kong

At Hang Fook Camp with Jackie Pullinger-To (1995)

Jackie and her husband John

By plane to Spain (1991) ...

Peter teaching at Arken, Sweden (1993)

Olive Stewart, Eva Dean and Bill Stewart, Associate Counsellors en-route to Switzerland, 1997 (below)

... with Peter and Carol Armon Horizon workers in Spain. Peter is a former member of the initial Advisory Board

Konrad and Monica Muller - former 9-Week students & Ellel representatives in Switzerland

Australia

Merroo Christian Centre near Sydney

Ken Curry, Director of 'Health Care in Christ', Australia

First Ellel visit to India (1995) with former 9-Week School student Pat Wakeham (rt)

Fiona Horrobin with Lynda Hicks who was wonderfully healed at Merroo (1996)

Jill Southern and Ken Hepworth with the Ghana ministry team (1997)

Ros Curry presenting thank you gifts to the team (1997)

Derek and Beryl Puffett (Telefriend Ministries) welcoming Peter and Fiona to South Africa (1998)

Attentive listeners at the Durban conference

Pastor's lunch at Cape Town

Worship at the Johannesburg conference

Sheila Bowditch (Glyndley) teaching at the Danish conference (1997)

Knut and Ruth Evensen - former 9-Week students and Ellel representatives in Denmark

Ellel Pierrepont

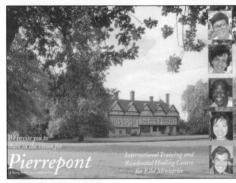

We invite you to share in the vision for
Pierrepont
A home waiting to minister
International Training and
Residential Healing Centre
for Ellel Ministries

Jill Southern,
Director of Ellel
Pierrepont, with her
husband Ron

Thanksgiving meeting for
the acquisition of
Pierrepont (1995)

NETS 3 and the
Pierrepont team (1998)

50 tons of
free carpet tiles
from Shell

Fred and Barbara Elgar

Ian Coates with 'Big
Bertha', the ancient
boiler and heating system
he and Basil Bird
successfully restored

Just some
of the treasure
recovered from
Tadley!

The Great Hall window

Staff dining room

The Main House in winter

Alona - Ukrainian YIP and now our main translator into Russian

Pierrepont Clock Tower

Ellel Ministries

6 MONTH INTERNATIONAL SCHOOL

NETS

Dynamic Training in

HEALING

DISCIPLESHIP

& EVANGELISM

Teaching in the Great Hall of Pierrepont

NETS 2 students

John Kilford presenting Oleg (Ukraine) with his NETS 2 certificate

Luke 9:11, the foundational Scripture of the ministry

"*Jesus welcomed the people, taught them about the Kingdom of God and healed those in need.*"

Luke 9:11

HANDBOOK

Ellel Grange
Glyndley Manor
Ellel Pierrepont

BRINGING THE HEART OF GOD TO THE HEART OF MAN

The Ellel Ministries Teaching Team (1998)

Peter and Fiona Horrobin

The Ellel Ministries team (1997)

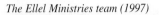

a hundred. Above this more accommodation for the Young Peoples Service Team could also be provided. Two houses right next door to the Manor came on the market for sale at the same time and it was decided to go ahead to purchase these for staff accommodation as well as the Manor.

Once again the team set out to share the vision for the ministry, this time in the south of the country. With a combination of gifts and loans the property was acquired in December 1991 and Glyndley Manor was added to the work. More importantly the vision that God had given Geoff Shearn ten years previously was a step closer to fulfilment.

Building the Team

Barry and Jan Jay, who had been the first wardens of Ellel Grange, temporarily moved into the Manor to supervise the building work and the preparation of the building for its new use. They also had the job of gathering together the nucleus of a team to run the new centre and to implant into that team the same heart for welcoming, teaching and healing that was at Ellel. It soon became clear that God had already prepared people of His choice for many of the key roles at Glyndley.

Joe and Ruth Hawkey, two of the original Associate Counsellors at Ellel Grange, and both gifted teachers, gave up their jobs to become the first leaders of the Glyndley team. Joe had management and engineering experience from industry and Ruth was a school teacher. They were joined by two other couples who moved to live nearby to form the first Leadership Team at Glyndley Manor: Pennant and Maureen Jones and Roy and Rosalind Keefe.

Pennant took early retirement from his work as a director of the Engineering Industry Training Board and Maureen came with many years of experience as a Doctor in General

Practice. She had left this two years previously knowing that God wanted her to give her time to a ministry of counselling. Both had served for many years as Bible class teachers and Pennant was a member of the General Synod of the Church of England. Roy had experience in accountancy and as a Church administrator and at the beginning had oversight of Glyndley's finances and bookstall. Rosalind had excellent secretarial skills, but her main task became the important one of co-ordinating all the prayer and intercessory activities associated with Glyndley.

Round this team of six, other key roles were filled by people clearly called by God to the work. Tony and Eileen Tack, also moved to live in Hailsham. Eileen was the first housekeeper and became a real mother to the team, while Tony became the manager of the estate and grounds. Tony had long sensed that before he retired he would have the opportunity to serve the Lord with his gardening skills. In the four years he was there the grounds of Glyndley were literally transformed from a jungle into picturesque parkland.

In the first weeks dense undergrowth of brambles was removed from the area above the lake, which was formerly invisible from the house. As this was cleared and spring came, carpets of snowdrops, daffodils and bluebells were revealed, which had been completely covered before. It was as if God was demonstrating something of what was to happen in the lives of hundreds of people who were to come to Glyndley Manor. Many have since testified of the blessing and sense of God's presence found in walking through the woodland and round the lake.

Looking back it is clear that God knew just what would be needed to take a new centre through its vital early days. The local knowledge of the area provided by Rita Goddard, the first administrator was invaluable. Steve Bland responded to the call to serve as the catering manager and moved from Cumbria, with Andrea and their daughters, to live at Glyndley. Under his care excellent food was always served and many others were trained by him.

Shirley Ansell, fluent in French and German, with years of experience in tourism, came as the first receptionist. Hermione Kaye and Roz Browne both joined at the start and still serve on the house staff. Both are unique and prayerful characters. Roz knew the Lord was calling her to serve in the laundry at Glyndley; she made it a house of prayer.

Ruth Dahl, a qualified Social Worker from Norway, had been at Ellel Grange for a time and came to join the staff. Together Ruth Hawkey, Maureen Jones and Ruth Dahl made an excellent team to organise the work of ministry and counselling for the courses and healing retreats. Just as the Ellel team did at the Grange, those at Glyndley prayed round the house and grounds claiming it and hallowing it all for God's work.

Glyndley Develops

Chapter 14 describes the nine-week *School of Evangelism, Healing and Deliverance* and records how the first of these was the opening event at Glyndley Manor in February 1992 . It was quite an undertaking for a new team, in a new centre, to commence operations with a packed nine-week programme of teaching and training; but God was in charge and the forty-three students loved it. They entered fully into everything and were largely unaware of the frequent improvisation that was going on behind the scenes as the team grappled with situations they had not faced before.

For Peter, also, it was a very testing time, because the school coincided with the latter stages of a long-term, in-depth ministry which proved impossible to put on hold. Joe and Ruth Hawkey, Barbara Baggaley, Pennant and Maureen Jones, and others played their part in keeping the School on track. The School ended with one testimony after another of people sharing what God had done for them while at Glyndley. For the team those testimonies were heard with great thanksgiving to God and an enormous sense of relief.

There have now been eight Schools at Glyndley. Each one has been uniquely different and greatly blessed by God. There are people now exercising important roles in the Body of Christ around the world who give thanks for their time at a Glyndley School. In addition it has been strategic in training some key people who are now exercising vital functions in all the Ellel centres.

As well as being the base for the School, Glyndley set about the task of being the Ellel Centre in the South. The original training courses followed the pattern set at Ellel Grange, but it was not long before Glyndley began to develop new courses of its own.

Early on the Leadership felt burdened by the number of people coming on Retreats with marriage problems. Out of this a new *Ministry to Marriage* course was designed and became a valuable feature of the Manor's programme, and was later used at Ellel Grange and in Canada.

Other innovations followed, including *Walking in Healing,* as a follow-up to Healing Retreats and a special course on *Healing for Women,* taught by women on the team. Other specialities were summer courses in German and French. Such outreach to continental Europe was part of the original vision for Glyndley.

Ken Hepworth, who had spent a number of years serving with the RAF in Germany, has led a German course in each of the past three years. This has now become a regular part of the programme. Pennant and Maureen led a similar course for twenty French-speaking people in 1996 and the hope is that this, too, will become a regular event.

Changes and Challenges

Joe and Ruth's time as leaders of Glyndley was, however, to be limited. They answered the call to go to Canada to be founder Directors of the work there. Ruth Dahl also went over to Canada to help in setting up a ministry office. Initially it was thought that their stay would be for a short period of six months, so Pennant Jones was appointed to be Acting Director in their absence.

As the months slipped by, however, it became increasingly clear that the Canadian task would be a longer one than first imagined, so Pennant assumed full responsibility for Glyndley Manor and Maureen became Ministry Manager. Under her leadership a ministry team of high quality was established and trained. Likewise she ensured that students on successive Schools were instructed in the best disciplines of counselling and ministry. Roy and Ros Keefe also became involved in in-depth prayer ministry.

When the Hawkeys and Ruth Dahl went to Canada, there was an immediate need to strengthen the team, but God knew beforehand of the needs. Ken Hepworth was seconded from Ellel Grange for a time as the staff speaker at Glyndley Manor, though it was not many months before he too was to be whisked away to Canada!

Two Associate Counsellors, David and Mary Rayner, were invited to join the team. They sold their furnishing business and, like others before them, moved home. David brought an exceptional organising ability which, combined with a real care for people, made him ideally suited to his job of Courses Manager. Mary had been a much-valued secretary at the Christian Medical Fellowship and was just the person to take over from Pennant as Administrator of the Schools.

One of the students on the first School was Sheila Bowditch, who had just completed eleven years of service aboard OM ships. She joined the team soon after finishing the school and was able to take over from Ruth Dahl in the Ministry Office.

Stretching the Team

Sometimes there seemed to be no quick answer to prayer for new staff. For example, for months prayer was asked for a worship leader but no answer came. Meanwhile the team did the best they could. Slowly it dawned that the answer to the prayer was already there. God wanted the latent talents He had already implanted in people on the team to be nurtured and used. This has been the Glyndley story again and again.

Shortly after Wendy Whitten, another ex-school student, had joined the team, a supporter donated all the components for a very large commercial glass house to the Manor. All that was needed was to erect it. Wendy was a trained Civil Engineer and her skill was just what was needed to make sure that the foundations were laid exactly as required. She was also a pianist, but had no experience of leading worship. Nevertheless, bit by bit, she developed to become a sensitive and accomplished musician and led worship effectively.

Paul Consadine joined the YPST and first picked up a guitar at Glyndley. What a joy it was to see him become a confident worship leader over a period. At the same time he was learning from Steve in the kitchen and became an excellent cook!

When Tony Tack retired a replacement to manage the grounds was needed. Mike and Lois Pursglove had for a long time felt called to the work, but Mike had suffered a severe motorcycle accident, breaking both his legs. It was thrilling to see prayer being answered as slowly but surely Mike exchanged his crutches for a walking stick and regained much of his former strength. In 1997, three years after his accident he was strong enough to shoulder the full responsibility for the grounds, with Lois and others in support.

When Rachel France first came, no one knew she could play the piano. First in the YPST meetings, then at staff prayers and finally in the Conference room we saw her gift emerging like a lovely flower. Mark Adamson and Jeremy Himsworth joined the Young Peoples team early on and served for over four years. Each of them became responsible junior managers and left with a new-found confidence that helped them to begin career training; Mark in accountancy and Jeremy as a teacher.

It was the same with the teachers. Step by step Pennant, Maureen and Sheila took on more and more teaching and became accomplished teachers on the courses and healing retreats. *Ministry to Marriage* became a speciality for Pennant and Maureen and a much-blessed course.

In 1995 David and Denise Cross, who had been at Ellel Grange for some time, were invited by the Executive Leadership to join the team at Glyndley. They had first entered the work after a Church Visit to their home village of Kincraig, in the Scottish Highlands.

During that weekend some people were deeply touched by God and David and Denise stayed up all night asking questions of Ho Tan Whai Aun, a much-loved Malaysian member of the Ellel Grange team with great skills in computers, ministry and building relationships!

David was an engineer and Denise a mathematics teacher. They came to Glyndley as Centre Managers and additional teachers for a period of eighteen months before taking over the Leadership from Pennant and Maureen when they retired from the work at Easter 1997. Under their Directorship the tradition of developing home talent has continued and more team members and Associate Counsellors have been drawn into teaching and speaking.

As the years have gone by more than seventy others from many nations have served at Glyndley, each making their own individual and valuable contribution to making it a place full of the love of God.

The Continuing Vision

When the work at Glyndley began, planning permission was sought and granted for an extension to the building. This was intended to be in two phases; the first to build a larger dining room, offices and staff room and the second, at a later stage, to add a large auditorium. In 1993 a campaign to raise funds for the first part was mounted and some £70,000 was raised. It was necessary to revise the plans in the light of experience and local authority approval was sought for the changes.

There was a strong temptation to use the funds available to lay the foundations for the extension, but as Director, Pennant felt it wise to wait until the planning permission was given.

Unaccountably, instead of taking weeks this took months and finally came through in August 1994. That was just a fortnight after a hidden outbreak of dry rot was discovered which triggered a major upheaval at Glyndley. For months staff had to contend with noise, dust and inconvenience as substantial parts of the Manor were ripped apart by contractors until all the active fungus was removed and the building treated.

With the consent of all the donors who could be contacted, the extension funds had to be used for the dry rot. Had the extension been started before the discovery of the rot, the situation would have been far worse. It was also just before the decision to acquire Pierrepont was taken, which could change the character of any extension to Glyndley. It was as though God knew the timing and held us back.

When the enormity of the dry rot problem became clear, Pennant recalls awaking during one night and sensing God saying *"Look at Isaiah 41 about half way down the left column on the page!"* In the morning he found these words *"Do not fear, for I am with you; do not be dismayed, for I am your God, I will strengthen you and help you."*

God certainly did help through a very difficult period and the staff responded to the need for extra effort and inconvenience magnificently. Bit by bit the affected parts of the Manor were brought back into use, in better shape than they were before.

There was one critical period when the whole of the east side of the top floor had to be exposed while a team of workers led by John Allen, from Ellel Grange, rebuilt the wall with new materials. For three whole weeks there was not a drop of rain and it was November! It rained the day after Will Ballantyne nailed down the last piece of felt making it water tight again.

God has clearly had his hand on Glyndley for a long time. Before a Manor was ever built there was a nunnery on the site and 250 years ago, in the early 1700s, a *"dissenting congregation"* was meeting at Glyndley! Praise to God in the building was again restored in 1986 when the four Christian families took it over, in the same month as Ellel Grange opened. As for the rest of Ellel Ministries, there remain chapters yet to be written about Glyndley Manor.

The vision is being fulfilled but is not yet complete. May be there is more to happen within the *"little houses"* of Geoff Shearn's vision. God has shown that He knows best what to do with Glyndley. We trust Him to continue to provide the people and funds that have enabled the Manor to be the warm and homely place of healing where so many have testified to the tangible and healing presence of the love of God.

CHAPTER 13

Visitors from Near and Far

Interest in the work of Ellel Ministries grew rapidly in the early days - especially as some well-known speakers began to teach special training courses at the Grange and take part in conferences. The demand for places at some of these courses meant that Ellel's facilities were inadequate for the numbers who wanted to attend. The upper lawns at the back of Ellel Grange were, however, ideally proportioned for the erection of a marquee that would seat several hundred people.

Graham Powell was the first person to use the marquee in April 1988. His teaching on deliverance opened people's eyes and helped them to see its relevance to the wider healing ministry. In November 1998 it was Bill Subritzky's turn. Bill was another speaker for whom the marquee was essential. Many people travelled from all over the country to learn from this New Zealand Anglican businessman, who had first learned about healing from the well-known healing evangelist, Harry Greenwood. But Bill is not an imitator of any man! God has developed in him a unique style and gifting which some would find very direct, but others would simply call authoritative.

Bill does not shrink from speaking the word of God uncompromisingly. He speaks forthrightly about even the most sensitive of subjects. When he speaks people certainly listen and are challenged to re-evaluate their lives in the light of Scriptural truth. His word of knowledge ministry, linked with evangelism is a unique blend of charismatic experience and old-fashioned Gospel preaching.

Next came Eric Delve. Eric was an unusual evangelist who had long recognised the need for healing and evangelism to be seen as compatible ministries. He and Peter had got to know each other in local missions during Mission England.

Eric's unique style of evangelism, and Ellel's concern to see young people discipled in the things of the Kingdom, resulted in special Youth Leaders Workshops at Ellel Grange in 1989 and 1990. These were followed by four nights of evangelism in the marquee when young people were brought by their Youth Leaders in car and coach from all over the North West. Many were to find faith in Christ at Ellel Grange during those few days of dynamic ministry. Eric is now an Anglican Minister in Maidstone, Kent.

Another regular visitor in the early days, and friend of the ministry was Marilyn Baker. Marilyn, as a singer who is blind, has an especially sensitive spirit and some of her songs have proved to be the most enduring and important that have ever been written in terms of their relevance to the healing ministry. Her tapes have often been played to people going through hard times of personal ministry. As Marilyn sings God speaks through her words right into the hearts and spirits of the wounded.

At Ellel she was always accompanied by her friend Tracy Williamson. Tracy is profoundly deaf, but again, like Marilyn, is very sensitive to God. It is as if her inability to hear people very well has made her especially sensitive to hearing God. The team will always be grateful to God for the enduring fellowship in the Kingdom that is part of the fruit of their visits to Ellel Grange.

One of the most influential and precious speakers to visit Ellel Grange was Tom Marshall. Tom was a quiet New Zealander with a remarkable teaching gift. His books on *Healing from the Inside Out, Relationships* and *Leadership* will remain Christian classics for many years to come. His conferences in the marquee were packed to capacity.

He was to make several visits to Ellel Grange and on each occasion crowds came to learn from his lifetime of Pastoral and Teaching experience. He had that unique gift of making you think he was only speaking to you. His tapes from those early visits are still listened to by those who appreciate the gift that Tom's wise teaching is to the Body of Christ. Perhaps his greatest gift to the ministry was his advice and guidance to the whole team at the 1992 Staff Conference.

It was Tom, also, who stressed to Peter that as the ministry grew people would come in and join the work who had not been able to share in the early pioneering days. They would not be familiar with the initial vision and history of the ministry. Tom said that it was absolutely essential for the whole team to be regularly reminded of the vision and purpose for which God had brought the work into being.

Tom's words were wise, and proved to be prophetic. For, over the years, one of the more difficult areas of ministry management has been keeping the team focussed on the vision and not allowing people to take the work in alternative directions. This book will ensure that future new members of the team will have a written record of how the work came into being and of some of the things that happened in the early days.

Tom was to have been one of the main speakers at *The Church Ablaze* conference at Brighton in October 1993. Sadly, in the summer of 1993, he was struck down with a brain tumour and before the conference could take place he was taken into the presence of the Lord. Peter flew out to Australia to pray with him during the latter weeks of his life. His widow, Gabriella Marshall, has remained a friend of the ministry and Peter and Fiona were pleased to enjoy fellowship with her in Sydney during the 1997 team visit.

Bob Gordon was another dynamic speaker who taught at Ellel Grange. His teaching on *Men of a Different Spirit* (Numbers 14:24) is still talked about, by those who were present, as having been of life changing significance. Joe Hawkey was particularly impacted by Bob's teaching, bringing him to a deeper point of surrender to God. Joe, and his wife Ruth, later joined the team and moved south as the first Directors of Glyndley Manor.

While he was at Ellel Grange Bob gave to Peter a particularly significant personal word. He saw Peter as a man who was walking forwards with what God had called him to do, but that ahead of him was a very big drop over the edge of a steep cliff. Bob told Peter that he might be tempted to hold back from pressing on in the ministry because of the cliff edge that lay ahead. But God was telling him not to slow down, but to keep on going and not to be afraid, because when you get to the very edge of the cliff, and only when you get there, you will see a stairway, carved in the rock, down which it will be safe for you to go.

There are several occasions since then when that prophetic word has been precisely fulfilled! It is interesting that Bob's earlier testimony of hanging on to God in the face of impossibilities, told in his book *Out of the Melting Pot,* had also been of great encouragement to Peter.

Tragically Bob was to die at the very early age of 53, towards the end of 1997. Bob's passing was a particular reminder to Peter that our days are not limitless and that it is so important we fulfil the purposes, for which God has called us to Himself, while there is yet time.

Glyndley Manor have also had their share of visitors, including Francis and Judith MacNutt. It was a packed centre that shared with them in a memorable training and ministry course.

Another couple with a specialised healing ministry, whose

encouragement and impact on the work has been significant, is John and Paula Sandford. They first visited at a time when the team were really struggling with major theological issues over some aspects of healing - especially in the area of deliverance. It was encouraging to find two people, whom God had called to a specialist ministry in inner healing, who, nevertheless, understood so thoroughly the need for deliverance and were willing to talk for long hours with the team to share their experiences and insights.

They taught a much appreciated week-long training course, but behind the scenes it was their gracious counsel, advice, help and support that spoke volumes to the team about the quality of their ministry. They have remained close friends of the work and recently conducted their three week training school at Pierrepont as part of the NETS 1 training programme.

Close friends of the Sandfords are Paul and Gretel Haglin. It was through their gracious influence that the Sandfords were encouraged to visit the Grange in the first place. During the first year of the ministry, David Barratt, one of the founder members of the Advisory Board, told the team about this unique couple with an unusual double ministry. *"They are very American"* (whatever that means) they were told, *"But what they say is very special."*

And special they have been. Their friendship, intercession, speaking and personal sharing has been one of the constant threads of encouragement throughout the history of the work. God joined their hearts with the leadership of the ministry on their first visit and the cords of love have never been broken. They have spoken at special training courses, taken holiday schools at both Glyndley Manor and Ellel Grange and addressed the whole team at the annual staff conferences. Now, also, they are regular visitors, teachers and supporters of the work at Ellel Canada.

They have been praying for a long time that God will open the doors to Ellel in the United States. It seems as though that day is drawing nearer as Ellel Canada assumes a wider role as the North American Headquarters of Ellel Ministries and not just the Canadian Centre.

Resurrection Christian Ministries is the name under which Paul and Gretel minister. They are an extremely mature couple, having walked with the Lord for many years and seen and experienced first-hand the growth of the charismatic renewal, sharing in both its joys and pitfalls. They have a special ministry to leaders, and in their itinerant work have a very particular gift of impartation of wisdom and counsel. Paul and Gretel have been personal friends and advisers to Peter and Fiona and there has been regular contact and prayer fellowship with them over the years. They are indeed 'fathers in the Lord' to the Leadership of the ministry.

In 1995 Peter and Fiona joined Paul and Gretel at their home with John and Paula Sandford. It was a special time for mutual sharing and encouragement. But during that week there was a particularly aggressive media onslaught on Ellel via a TV programme. God knew what he was doing, however, in having Peter and Fiona there at that particular time. John Sandford's prophetic voice encouraged them to *"be at peace, for no man can close down God's voice - in time, God's voice will come out clearer"*. His gentle advice helped them to trust that the Lord will let His voice be heard through those who have been healed and have a testimony to tell of what God has done for them. One day their voice will be heard more fully.

CHAPTER 14

The Schools Develop

Assessing the Need

At first the thought of having students in residence for nine weeks sent shock waves through the team. The first courses at Ellel Grange had been for one day only. Then there were the 48-hour courses spread over three days. As the team gained more experience five day and one week courses were introduced into the programme. But nine weeks, surely not!

Almost since day one of the ministry, however, there had been people knocking on the door and asking to stay for longer periods of time. They didn't just want to come for a short course. They wanted to stay longer and gain more experience in ministering to people. They wanted to ask question after question about the theology which underpinned the ministry. They needed time to study the Scriptures and see for themselves just what the Bible had to say - not just about healing, but about the much wider topic of discipleship which is so closely linked to healing.

A Doctor and his wife came to stay for three weeks. Greg and Merle were from Australia. As a Doctor Greg knew that not all medical problems could be solved through medical means. While they were at Ellel Grange, God not only broadened their horizons of understanding, but brought deep healing to them personally. Greg, especially, went home a different man. Seven years later he still talks about what God did for him at Ellel Grange. Back home in Sydney Greg and Merle have diligently applied all the lessons they learnt and are now deeply involved in the healing ministry.

Bruce Boynes, a Baptist minister from South Africa, took a sabbatical away from his Church to study counselling. After eight weeks of study in the States he was suffering from the frustration of having acquired a lot of knowledge but not having any real answers as to how to help people in a practical way. He headed for Ellel Grange for a 'flying visit' on his way home. He stayed for three weeks.

The first thing God did was to challenge him in the realm of the spirit. He shook his head, almost in disbelief as he was filled with the Spirit and began to exercise the gifts of the Spirit. His conservative background told him that these things should not be happening today. His eyes and his ears told him differently!

He counselled a man with another member of the team. The time came for ministry. It was clear that the man needed deliverance, but would the demons respond to Bruce's authority? Bruce was excited to discover that the authority Jesus had given him was sufficient for the situation. He reluctantly went home after three weeks of training on the job. Since then God has been using Bruce to counsel and bring healing to many others - especially other Pastors and leaders.

Maureen was also a Doctor. As a spirit-filled Christian she knew that God was able to heal, but there was much to learn about how to apply the truths of Scripture into the lives of broken and hurting people. She took a short sabbatical from her practice and shared, especially, in some in-depth ministries to very hurting people. She saw first-hand the reality and need for deep inner-healing as well as deliverance ministry. When Maureen and her husband Pennant later retired they moved to Sussex to be part of the team at Glyndley Manor. They were to play a major role in the development and leading of 9-week training Schools.

These and many other people all wanted more than could be offered on a weekend at Ellel Grange or a one-week training course. They needed more teaching and more opportunities to put the teaching into practice. The team put together, therefore, a tentative programme for a longer period of training.

First there would be four weeks of intensive teaching. Then a week off to assimilate all that had been learnt - after that personal ministry for each of the students, as well as nearly three weeks of sharing with the regular ministry teams on Healing Retreats. And right at the end there would be a final week of teaching - nine weeks in all.

The leadership were uncertain. Would anyone want to come for so long. Could they afford to pay the fees that would be necessary to sustain the overheads of a centre? Where should it be held?

The First Schools

The imminent Brighton Conference provided an ideal opportunity to test the waters. A leaflet was hurriedly produced and made available at the conference. As a result there were dozens of enquiries, many from overseas. The idea of a School certainly seemed viable. Its location was to be solved by the opening of Glyndley Manor. Glyndley would be the home of the first *International School of Evangelism, Healing and Deliverance.*

Joe and Ruth Hawkey, the first Directors of Glyndley Manor, certainly had their hands full, but they and the rest of the pioneer team rose magnificently to the occasion. On that first school were fifteen Canadians, as well as students from thirteen other countries. It was a truly international blend of people who descended on the Manor for that pioneering event.

But the students had little knowledge of the nervous apprehension there was behind the scenes! At the end of the School, however, there were some quite exceptional testimonies from the students as to what God had done in their lives. God used the School to help a number of them to understand new directions God was wanting them to take - including Sheila Bowditch, who joined the team and is now the Ministry Manager at Glyndley Manor.

By the end of 1998 there had been fourteen 9-week schools, nine at Glyndley Manor and five in Canada. Every one has been unique. Whilst the teaching content has been very consistent, each has had its own particular flavour provided by the international mix. Many deep and lasting friendships have been formed - including subsequent marriages!

Students from a total of over forty nations have gone back to their own countries to apply the truths they have learned. Many of them are in full-time Christian work. There are ex-9 week students working in Nepal, India, Pakistan, Sri Lanka, Thailand, Malaysia, Singapore, Hong Kong, Japan, Philippines, Australia, New Zealand, USA, Canada, Denmark, Sweden, Norway, Holland, Germany, Finland, Spain, France, Switzerland, Austria, Russia, Belarus, Hungary, Poland, Ukraine, Romania, Uganda, Kenya, Burundi, South Africa, Zimbabwe, Ghana, Nigeria and Mexico - as well as England, Scotland, Ireland and Wales.

Living Fruit

Two ladies who got to know each other at Glyndley, but who had no idea that their subsequent paths would be so similar, were Donna Parachin and Jill Southern. Both their lives were irreversibly changed by the experience. As Jill was heard to say on a later occasion, *"Going on a school can seriously damage your future!"* - for the better!

For Donna, leaving behind her husband Al in Canada was a very major step. But he survived the ordeal and Donna was very deeply impacted by what she learned. It was the first time that she had heard teaching and seen ministry that could effectively deal with the consequences of the real-life problems which she and Al had experienced as teenagers. They had both been wonderfully saved out of the street-scene of the sixties. Al subsequently became a pastor and is currently the President of the Christian Broadcasting Associates in Canada (700 Club).

Donna was one of thirteen Canadians who were on the second school. Donna, who was active in Christian leadership and with a successful business career behind her, was later to join the team at Ellel Canada and subsequently became the first Canadian Director of the Centre.

For Jill, leaving Ron at home for nine weeks was not so much of a problem. He was only sixty miles away and the journey home was quite manageable at weekends. But the impact on Jill was nonetheless equally dramatic. To go on the school Jill had taken very early retirement from her senior management role with Thorn EMI. God worked miracles in the company to make it possible. She was wondering what God had in store for her and Ron in the future.

Not even the School could have prepared her for becoming the founding Director of Ellel Ministries' physically largest Centre, though without the teaching she had absorbed so enthusiastically at Glyndley Manor it would have been impossible for her to do the job.

From School after School have come testimonies of people from around the world about the impact the teaching and ministry experience has made on their lives. It has brought healing to their past and equipped them for their future.

In Switzerland Antoinette Schramm gathered people together to pray that God would touch her nation and bring healing to the Swiss people. Slowly interest grew and as a result of her prayers the doors opened for German language teaching conferences in northern Switzerland. Before long there will be a German language centre. Antoinette is now with the Lord, but the legacy of her prayers lives on.

In Malaysia Anglican Priest Vincent Lau, and his wife Orwan, took the content of the School, adapted it to his own culture and began to put on weekend training courses. St.Gabriel's Church has become well-known in Kuala Lumpur for the teaching and training that is available there.

In Madras (India) Kevin and Deborah Kamilraj took the teaching to the poor and deprived people whom God had called them to work amongst. God did wonderful things as they taught the foundational principles of healing and discipleship. As a result a significant local ministry has now developed.

In New Zealand Tony and Raewyn Bartholomew have similarly taken the material and applied it to their local situation at Tauronga. And the notes of the complete school are now being translated into Russian in readiness for the first Russian language School, which is currently being planned for 1999.

One dimension to the Schools, which has had far-reaching ramifications in the way foundational truths are communicated, is the development of new teaching illustrations through the cut and thrust of question and answer sessions which the school environment permits. One day, when Peter was getting to grips with the theology of salvation and explaining the present need for healing through Jesus's finished work on the cross, he used whatever was available on the lunch table to illustrate his point.

Among other things an orange was used to represent the spirit, and two apples to represent the flesh - the soul and the body. These were used to illustrate aspects of the reality of the spiritual battle that each Christian has to fight on a daily basis, as described by Paul in Romans 7:14-20, and which can be expressed as the war between the will of the spirit and the will of the soul. This teaching has been developed as *"the Gospel of apples and oranges"* and has been used with powerful effect at many of the Ellel teaching conferences. Other ways of expanding foundational teaching, in a way that is both profound and simple, have been strategic in making people aware of the importance of discipleship as well as the personal relevance of healing and deliverance.

There are many remarkable stories which could be told of how students found the funds to go on the school. God has used everything from businesses that were suddenly sold to gifts that came, as it were, from nowhere to pay the way. It seems that once people have committed themselves to move forward in faith that God then brings release of the necessary resources.

The 9-week School is now a firmly established component of the Ellel Teaching Programme, but such are the difficulties for some students, with regard to getting a sufficiently long period of time away from work or family, that the Canadians have pioneered a modular version whereby students can tackle the School in four two-week slots. The formula may change according to personal circumstances and local situations, but the content remains much the same.

Some students, however, wanted more! They had learned so much on the schools, that they now wanted to spend more time learning how to put the teaching into practice. At a later date Pierrepont, a country estate near Farnham in

Surrey, was acquired for this purpose. This is now the home of the 6 Month Training School known as NETS - **N**ine **E**leven **T**raining **S**chool. Luke 9:11 is the foundational Scripture for the ministry.

The nine week syllabus was expanded to provide more time to assimilate the material and many more subjects were added to the programme. Visiting teachers such as Jim Graham, David Noakes and Chua Wee Hian have added much to the teaching content. And with more time for practical ministries and training in evangelism the NETS School has a unique place within the Ellel programme.

CHAPTER 15

Ellel Canada

Singing Waters

Among those who attended the *The Battle Belongs to the Lord* at Brighton, and the subsequent conference at Budapest, were John and Carol Arnott (Pastors of what was then the Airport Vineyard, Toronto) and a fellow Vineyard Pastor Paul White, with his wife Sandie. They, and other Canadians who had also been at Brighton, liked what they saw and wanted to know more. As a result John invited Peter and a team to Canada in 1991 for the *Deliverance Ministry Training Course* at *Singing Waters,* a Christian Retreat Centre about an hour's drive north of Toronto.

The conference was filled to capacity with people from many different Churches and some very profound ministries took place. One lady who was prayed for confessed to having hated her fourth daughter. She had not wanted to be pregnant again and wished her daughter dead. The daughter was, nevertheless, safely delivered. It was nearly forty years later, at *Singing Waters,* that she repented and was delivered of demonic power that had been given rights in her life through the hatred in her heart. Peter also felt led to pray for the daughter, that she should be set free of anything that had been controlling her because of her mother's hatred, knowing that hatred and death are very closely related.

On a later visit to Toronto, in 1993, this same lady came running up to Peter waving a photograph of her baby grandson, Alex. Alex had recently been born to the daughter who had formerly been hated. When Peter had prayed for the lady the previous year he did not know that her daughter was still childless after fourteen years of marriage. When her mother repented, her daughter had been set free from the curse of death and she was then able to conceive.

It was the teaching and fruit like this from the first conference at *Singing Waters* that led so many Canadians to decide to go to England for the 9-week *School of Evangelism, Healing and Deliverance* at Glyndley Manor. During the year that followed some of the Canadians who had been on the school were influential on the Board of *Singing Waters.* They shared with the rest of the Board about what they had seen of the work of Ellel Ministries. Among these were Jean Knox, then the Executive Director of *Singing Waters* and Gord Burrows, who became Chairman of the Board, with his wife Lorraine.

Singing Waters had been acquired in 1956 by a remarkable woman of faith called Kay Golbeck. She had been dramatically healed herself on at least two occasions and had an indomitable spirit. What she bought at first was an old farmhouse together with 47 acres of varied land. She set up a Charitable Trust to own and run the property and began to establish the estate as a Christian Retreat Centre.

The building was extensively added to over the years so that by the time she died it was able to accommodate up to fifty guests for residential retreats and training courses. The new extensions also incorporated a teaching room in the basement and a new dining room with kitchen facilities. In the years that followed her death a number of different ministries rented the building from time to time, including John Wimber, YWAM, and the Elijah House ministry of John and Paula Sandford.

After Kay's death, however, the remaining team continued to experience some of the same problems that had troubled the work over many years. Perhaps they did not have Kay's determination to overcome them or maybe they lacked vision and purpose of their own, but, for whatever reason, slowly and surely the ministry began to run down and financial difficulties loomed ahead. More particularly, the ministry to the troubled and hurting, which had been Kay Golbeck's founding mission, was shrinking and there were not enough finances available to cover the cost of doing the work for which *Singing Waters* had been established.

It was concerns such as these that led the Board to discuss the possibility of inviting Ellel Ministries to Canada. They came to a place of agreement over this and a telephone call was made to Peter at Glyndley Manor during the second 9-week School. *"Would Ellel Ministries like to consider taking over Singing Waters and establishing a North American ministry?"* came the voice over the phone. It was not a question that either Peter or the UK Leadership had previously considered although, when the team had been at *Singing Waters,* some of them had the strange feeling that one day soon they would be back!

Whilst it took a bit of time for the matter to be thought and prayed through, the UK Board of Ellel Ministries and the Canadian Board of *Singing Waters* eventually resolved the problems associated with establishing Ellel Ministries in Canada. A legal way forward was pioneered by Terry Carter, an outstanding Christian lawyer whose offices were, conveniently, just down the road in Orangeville.

Through the generosity of the Board *Singing Waters* became Ellel Canada in November 1993. It is recorded in some of Kay Golbeck's notes that the Lord had shown her that one day *Singing Waters* would be a place to which people would come for training from all over the world.

Ken Reeves, a member of the current Ellel Canada Board, and his wife Lorraine are a couple whose experience and memory span most of the years that Kay Golbeck was at *Singing Waters.* They remember her sharing her vision for the nations. Through Ellel Canada that aspect of her vision is being fulfilled. Ken and Lorraine also remember many of the spiritual battles Kay had to face at *Singing Waters*. It had not been an easy time for her. One of the first things to be initiated by the Ellel team was the work of claiming the ground (see, also, Chapter 5). They sought to deal with any spiritual powers that were affecting the land and opposing the work God had called into being through Kay Golbeck and which was now being continued by Ellel Ministries.

It took nearly three years for that process to be completed. Ken and Lorraine Reeves are convinced that the recent blessing on the ministry at Ellel Canada, in terms of spiritual unity and relationships with other Christian groups in the town of Orangeville, is a direct result of that work having been done. Kay battled for nearly thirty years to develop such relationships, but largely without apparent success, but God is faithful.

The Canadian Team Develops

A new Centre had, of course, to be led and staffed. Who could take on such a task at short notice? Joe and Ruth Hawkey were the obvious choice, but they had only been in charge at Glyndley for just twelve months. Could Glyndley stand the strain of losing its leaders to Canada so soon after the work had started? It was not an easy decision, and there were consequences, but Joe and Ruth accepted the challenge and moved to Orangeville to establish Ellel Ministries in Canada and set up a North American base for the ministry. They initially came by way of secondment from Glyndley Manor for a period of six months and kept up their responsibility for the Glyndley team from a distance - an arrangement which was far from ideal and which, with hindsight, the Ellel leadership could perhaps have handled better.

They set about the task of recruiting and training a ministry team and very quickly their quality teaching and experience began to be appreciated by the Canadians. But it was also soon obvious that it was going to take more than six months to see the work established. They stayed on considerably beyond their initial expectation; built up an excellent team of Associate Counsellors and developed good personal relationships with some of the local Churches. The ministry in Canada was on its way.

Then Joe and Ruth came to a point in their lives when God was saying to them that their present season with Ellel was coming to an end and that they were to lay down their responsibilities and wait on the Lord for a period. There was no break in relationship but they knew they had to go home to prepare for a new season in their life. In that season God has opened up for them a ministry in many local Churches as well as with other Christian organisations, but they are still regular teachers also at all of the Ellel Centres.

New Leadership

The Canadian team did not know how to respond to the news of Joe and Ruth's departure and, once again, emergency action had to be taken to put someone in charge of the ministry in Canada. Whilst there were emergent Canadian leaders, it was premature for one of them to be in a position to take on the role of Centre Director. Further reinforcements from the UK were still needed.

After Joe and Ruth's departure from Glyndley Manor for Canada, there had been an urgent need for a new teacher there. After a short period working in a local Church, Ken Hepworth had recently come back into the Ellel team, and was ready for more responsibility. He was an excellent teacher and had a lot of ministry experience. He and Jean stepped into the breach and moved to Glyndley Manor.

But no sooner had they established themselves there than the new vacancy occurred in Canada. A strong leader was urgently needed to maintain the momentum in Canada and keep the work on track. Ken and Jean packed their bags once again and, this time, journeyed over 3,000 miles to their new location for a two year period in charge.

The rest of the Canadian team also needed strengthening. At that time Steve and Barb Chua were growing in ability and authority within the work and they needed a fresh challenge. Barb is American and some of her family lived in Cleveland, only a few hours drive from Toronto and they believed the move to Canada was God's leading for them as a family. So Steve and Barb, with baby Joshua, joined the transatlantic pilgrimage and set up home at Ellel Canada.

A new leadership team soon evolved for the Canadian work with Ken Hepworth as Executive Director and Donna Parachin as his assistant. Martin Frankena, a gentle giant of a man, and Steve Chua completed the leadership team. They were all learning and the experience of working and sharing together in Canada proved to be an excellent training and development ground for each of them.

Though he was new to Ellel Ministries, Martin Frankena soon caught the heart of the vision and his teaching gift quickly developed to meet the needs of the situation. His sensitivity and gentleness was especially appreciated by those who were hurting - especially on the Healing Retreats.

In spite of all the personnel changes in the pioneering stages of the work, Ellel Canada was growing quickly in momentum and influence. Canada developed its own 9-week training schools as well as a comprehensive programme of shorter courses and Healing Retreats.

Forays began to be made into the USA also, largely as a result of invitations from people who had been on the Schools, Training Courses and conferences. Excellent relationships were also being developed with a number of local Church leaders, especially with Don Fitchett, Pastor of Orangeville Baptist Church.

Canadian Leadership

Ken and Jean's two years in Canada were completed in the spring of 1997. Ken was needed back in England as the next Director of Ellel Grange, following the retirement of Jim Russell. There was no-one else from England to fill the gap, but even if there had been someone available, the UK Executive Leadership would not have released them. For the time had come for Joe and Ruth's vision to be fulfilled of the work coming under Canadian Leadership.

Ever since she had been on the School at Glyndley Manor it was clear that God's hand for leadership had been on Donna Parachin. She is a natural leader, with a powerful teaching gift (especially in the area of intercession and spiritual warfare) and she and her husband are much respected leaders in the Canadian Christian community. Both the UK Executive and the Canadian Board were unanimous in inviting her to take on the job.

September 1997 saw the Canadian team hosting *The Battle Belongs to the Lord* at the local large Baptist Church. This event was unusual in that the conference was sponsored by about twelve local Pastors who had seen the developing work of Ellel Ministries at the local centre, and who wanted their own members to benefit from the teaching. Much of the foundational teaching was illustrated with drama. This style of presentation has a powerful effect in getting the message across and has added a significant dimension to the kind of training Ellel provides.

The effect on the local community has been significant as Pastors have begun to work together in a new way, recognising that God will bless their fellowships far more richly when the leaders are praying for each other and working together in unity.

Most of the Churches involved reported that there had been some very significant healings or ministries to key individuals in their congregations. The wife of an elder of one Church was baptised in the Holy Spirit on the first day, delivered of the consequences of freemasonry (which had often left her with a feeling of blackness and depression) on the second day and on the third day was healed of a chronic neck condition, following whip-lash injury in a car accident nine years previously! Her husband was well-placed to testify to what God had done. He is the local Doctor!

In September 1998 *The Church Ablaze* conference followed up the success of *The Battle Belongs to the Lord.* Once again there was tremendous blessing as God spoke deeply into the lives of those present, including many pastors and leaders from both Canada and the USA.

Ellel Canada is now well-established in the Canadian Christian scene with an increasing respect and appreciation of the ministry coming from right across the denominational spectrum. Their vision is not just restricted to Canada, however, for they are truly looking far afield as they seek God for future direction. Requests for training courses and conferences in the States are indicative of a growing interest in the work in the USA.

The potential for the ministry in North and South America is only just beginning to be realised. The Canadian team have tremendous vision and already they have made a strategic contribution to the overall development of the work. No doubt, in due course, a subsequent book will be written regarding God's dealings with the work of Ellel Ministries in Canada and the Americas.

CHAPTER 16

"Into All the World"

and other conferences

In many ways *The Battle Belongs to the Lord* conference in 1990 had the effect of taking the work of Ellel Ministries into the world-wide arena. There were many people there from other nations and, as a result, invitations to teach and minister overseas began to be received. The re-run of this conference in 1991 was immediately followed by teaching the same material in Budapest to delegates from 13 different Eastern European nations.

In October 1993 the teaching material was expanded beyond the horizons of healing and deliverance with *The Church Ablaze,* also held at the Brighton Centre.

The Church Ablaze was designed as a special teaching conference to inform and strengthen the Church. Teaching showed how the Church must be built up and equipped for doing the works of the Kingdom, for God requires His Church to be relevant, challenging, inspiring and ready for action. In May 1995 *The Church Ablaze* was followed by *The Day of His Power.*

During 1993 and 1994 the team made important trips to Malaysia and Hong Kong. Many friends were made as first, in 1993, the *Deliverance Ministry Training Course* was taught at Rawang, near Kuala Lumpur, at the invitation of Wong Kim Kong, then the Director of Malaysia Care, followed by teaching conferences in Hong Kong at both St Andrew's Church and Hang Fook Camp with Jackie Pullinger-To.

As a result of these visits to Kuala Lumpar a number of Malaysians attended the 9-Week *School of Evangelism, Healing and Deliverance* at Glyndley Manor. Among these were Vincent Lau (Anglican Vicar of St. Gabriel's, Kuala Lumpar), Florence Wang, Linda Tang and for part of the School, Stephen Goh. These formed the nucleus of a very committed group of prayer supporters who have met regularly ever since and been a constant encouragement to the ministry.

The 1994 trip included teaching conferences at the Full Gospel Assembly in Kuala Lumpur, at the SIB Church in Sabah (the former North Borneo) and further teaching conferences in Hong Kong at both St.Andrew's and Hang Fook Camp. It was exciting to see how some of the lessons that had been learned back at Ellel Grange produced ministry keys that were of powerful significance in ministering to some of the ex-prostitutes and drug addicts at Hang Fook Camp.

Whilst in Hong Kong, Fiona ministered to Becky Trask, an American Baptist missionary. She had been chronically ill with ME (chronic fatigue syndrome) for seven years. Her whole life was controlled by the symptoms which limited her activities to an absolute minimum of physical effort. Frequently she was so exhausted that she was only able to manage a few hours out of bed during the day and was in constant thirst, always having to carry around with her a glass of water.

The keys to her healing had been learnt behind the scenes at Ellel Grange, in hundreds of hours of ministry to individuals with very deep needs. The following day Becky was a transformed person, even taking part in a physically gruelling trip into China, prayer walking round one of the border cities. That one day's ministry had transformed Becky's life.

In 1995 Jackie Pullinger-To, with her husband John, made a return trip to the United Kingdom. Jackie was the main speaker at *Into All the World,* the October 1995 Ellel International Conference, at Blackpool.

Jackie's teaching had a great impact on both the Ellel team and the Conference delegates, laying down a challenge to the Body of Christ to be willing to die to oneself that others may live. Her radical understanding of Kingdom living is not a popular message in the west, though once having heard it, it is unforgettable, deeply moving, very challenging and life-changing.

The beginning of 1996 saw the opening up of German speaking Switzerland for a preliminary teaching conference. There was tremendous fruit and this was followed up with *The Battle Belongs to the Lord* being taken to Weinfelden in 1997.

Also in 1997 Jill Southern and Ken Hepworth took a team to Ghana for the first African conference. They returned full of thanksgiving to God for an amazing time, together with armfuls of invitations to return as soon as possible. There were many testimonies of what God had done in people's lives during the visit.

Knut and Ruth Evensen went on the 9-week school at Ellel Canada. They had a big heart for the hurting and had been Pastoring a city centre Church in Copenhagen for a number of years. Their positive experience of the teaching and personal ministry led them to invite a team to visit their Church in Denmark the following year for what proved to be a challenging and door-opening conference.

The tenth anniversary of the acquisition of Ellel Grange was partially celebrated by the first team visit to Australia. The Australian trip was divided into two halves. The first conference, at Melbourne, called *Jesus Frees,* was coordinated by John Ouw, a remarkable Chinese psychiatrist with the courage to speak out in his profession for the Christian healing ministry.

Such was the impact of this conference that two people packed their bags at once and flew straight to Glyndley Manor for the 9-week School that was just about to begin! Since the School these students have themselves been involved in their own ministries in other places.

The Sydney Conference, sponsored by *Health Care in Christ,* and organised by Ken and Ros Curry, was a more specialist event, being attended by a wide range of Christian Medics and Health Care Professionals, Pastors and Counsellors. It was here that Lynda Hicks, whose testimony was published in the Ellel Newsletter, was so wonderfully healed.

Lynda was a Christian nurse, but it was nearly three years since she had been able to work full-time because of her disability. She attended the Conference more out of a sense of duty, as a nurse, than in any expectation that she might be healed.

Two and a half years previously she had fallen off a cliff and broken her back in four places. Now she was a walking cripple - in constant pain, suffering severe side-effects from her permanent medication, a victim of chronic fatigue, depressed, suicidal, registered disabled and working through the legal consequences of the accident. Life seemed pointless.

But during that conference God met her in a quite extraordinary way and at a very deep level. Not only did she go home radically healed, but her relationship with God was totally transformed. Most of those present at the conference were members of the various medical professions. They had watched in awe as over a two hour prayer and ministry time God dealt with many different things and worked a miracle in her life.

Twelve months later, radiant and full of life, she told the remarkable story of her healing at the second Ellel Conference in Sydney. Such was the extent of her healing that she had just completed a tour of duty as the ship's nurse aboard the Operation Mobilisation vessel *Doulos* - a challenging task for even the fittest of fit people, let alone for someone whose back had been broken in four places and who had almost been given up for dead!

God touched so many people through this, and the Melbourne conferences, that fifteen Australians immediately applied to go to Pierrepont for the first 6-month NETS training school.

Ken Curry reported on the second conference in the *Health Care in Christ* Newsletter in the following words:

"The conferences that we have sponsored with Ellel Ministries in the last 2 years have seen the words of Luke 10 come to fruition. Evangelism, healing and deliverance have come together in an exciting and powerful way. We are seeing our mission statement come into being *'to see these people restored to wholeness in body, mind and spirit through the resurrection power of Jesus Christ.'* We are seeing more of what health care *'in Christ'* truly is.

"The Ellel conferences have been a great blessing to many who have received personal ministry but even more importantly, the Lord is releasing effective ministry into the Body of Christ. My life and my practice will never be quite the same.

"As I sat listening to the foundational teaching series and experienced the ministry times, a number of aspects became apparent to me. The first was that this teaching has an intensely Biblical foundation. The second was that the teaching and ministry were having very significant effects in people's lives. The third was that Biblical truth was being applied to ministry with a greater degree of understanding of what was happening in the spiritual realm than I had seen previously.

"Although I had previously heard the foundational teaching, I found that God was speaking to me regarding the truth and power of His word, and how fundamental it is for effective ministry to be grounded in the ministry of Jesus and the apostles. Something was happening in me which I had known in my head before, but was now releasing me to minister in the Spirit to a greater degree than I had known before.

"I was beginning to see why Peter Horrobin is so insistent that people first have the foundational teaching before going onto more specific teaching in other areas. Although in a sense we all know these teachings, I feel that we do not grasp their power to heal and set free. It is very exciting to know that we can truly minister to people just as Jesus did. It is not new techniques that we need, so much as an understanding of who we are in Christ, and the power of His Spirit within us to touch a hurting world."

In 1995 a small team made an exploratory trip to South Africa. One of the people Peter and Fiona met while they were there was Derek Puffett, the National Director of Telefriend Ministries. Telefriend is a national Christian telephone counselling service and help line organisation, currently having twelve centres in South Africa. The ministry was first established by Derek and Beryl in November 1986, just four weeks after Ellel Grange had been acquired.

Derek and Beryl made a subsequent visit to Ellel Grange to find out more about the ministry. As a result Derek invited a team to visit South Africa in 1998 for a series of teaching and training conferences in Cape Town, Durban and Johannesburg.

The primary objective of the visit was to extend the training of the telephone counsellors and assist them with face-to-face counselling opportunities. But many other people came as well, from a wide variety of different churches, and what God did over these conferences has established a major foundation for future developments in South Africa and the southern part of the African continent.

The interest in the work of Ellel Ministries overseas is growing rapidly and 1998 has seen the establishment of a new Overseas Division to co-ordinate future invitations and to watch over and encourage the expansion of the ministry to wherever God opens the doors.

Into All the World - via the Internet!

The work of Ellel Grange was first made known via word of mouth, correspondence and a Newsletter. The information in the Newsletter encouraged both prayer and action and as a result the work gradually became more well-known and established.

Over the years the Newsletter has been published about three times a year, according to the need to share information about the work and to inform people about forthcoming events. The Newsletter has been a vital bridge between the in-house team and supporters of the ministry. It has also provided an opportunity to publish some of the testimonies of what God has done in the lives of people touched by Him through the various activities of the ministry.

In the past few years a new form of publicity has hit the world. The Internet has literally exploded into significance as a means of making updated information constantly available - not just when it is possible to publish a Newsletter and not just within a very limited area of the world. The Internet is here to stay. It can be accessed for minimal cost from any country in the world and the information is instantly available.

Ellel Canada has made a significant contribution to the world-wide ministry of Ellel by pioneering the Internet as a means of providing basic information about the work in a readily accessible and attractively presented way. The Ellel Ministries Web page can be accessed via **www.ellelministries.org** and it is constantly being amended so that information about courses and conferences is always right up to date.

CHAPTER 17

On the Cutting Edge

Throughout the years of Ellel Ministries the work has had many different dimensions to it. There has always been the advertised public programme of training courses, conferences and healing retreats. There have also been many unadvertised team visits to local Churches up and down the land. Then there has been a continuous series of overseas visits, generally to conduct teaching conferences in places as far apart as Bergen and Johannesburg, or Atlanta City and Hong Kong.

The very heart of the ministry, however, has always been behind the scenes and out of the public eye, where hurting and broken people are loved back to life and healed. It has been through ministering to these people that the most important lessons have been learned, which have subsequently been taught on the training courses and conferences with such powerful effect.

In Ezekiel 34 we are urged to take care of the weak, heal those who are sick, bandage those who are hurt, bring back those who have wandered off and look for those who are lost. In Matthew's Gospel Jesus uses the parable of the lost sheep to encourage us to look for those that are lost, and in John 10 he describes himself as the Good Shepherd who is willing to die for the sheep. Scripture uses the picture of hurting sheep to turn our hearts to the needs of God's hurting children.

Ever since the work began there have always been such people at Ellel Grange. Sometimes they have stayed for days, at other times people have been there for weeks on end and even for longer periods. Some have come from backgrounds of terrible abuse - like the girl who at age 23 had not slept on a bed for twenty years through fear of what might happen to her on it. The floor under the bed was the only safe place for her. Others had come from backgrounds in the occult and because of what had happened to them were both very demonised and very hurting. Others were very broken or had come from psychiatric care without any real hope of ever again living a normal life.

But can one ever say that there is anyone that God is not able to heal or about whom He does not care? Never. The team have always approached every problem that they have had to face, therefore, with the same belief that, in God, there has to be an answer - even when humanly speaking the situation has been utterly hopeless. As a result many vital lessons have been learned which have subsequently been applied into the lives of others.

At times mistakes have been made, but when the heart attitude towards God (of those ministering and those receiving ministry) is right, then it is easy to back-track from false avenues and start again. This is not so easy if, perhaps, the one receiving ministry is only focussed on dealing with symptoms as opposed to establishing godly order in every area of their life. A desire to walk in obedience to God, come what may, is the most important foundation which the team would now seek to see established in people *before* commencing ministry. Without this there is likely to be the recurrence of a further problem sooner or later.

Healing the Broken Hearted

On a recent special Healing Retreat, 27 people, most of whom the team had formerly been unable to help significantly, were brought together for a period of ten days.

The objective of the retreat was to see what God would do if, instead of ministering intently into their problems, the focus of the retreat was initially on establishing God's order in their lives. The teaching, therefore, was aimed at putting down godly foundations of right beliefs and dealing with unforgiveness, bitterness, sin etc. at a much deeper level than had been possible in earlier ministries or on their Healing Retreats.

For a very significant number of those people it was the turning point in their lives. One lady came to the retreat straight from residential psychiatric care. She never went back. On the way towards her healing, however, she had to get to the point where her relationship with God was more important to her than her healing.

Another lady risked receiving love for the first time as God broke through the barriers she had placed around her hurting heart. It was a life transforming experience. With many of these people there was a need for much deliverance, but deliverance in itself, without the in-depth healing of the hurts and wounds of the past, is not enough. With some the battle for their very lives has been intense. For all there has been the need to press on into God, trusting him even when everything seems lost. And in every case we have found that the most important issues have only been resolved when matters of faith and relationship with God have been faced and overcome.

In recent years the team has done much work with people whose very personalities have been broken through the traumas and experiences of life. People who have been without hope. People whose only prospect for life was, at best, permanent drug medication or, at worst, institutionalisation in psychiatric care. For these, too, in Christ there is an answer.

When a person such as this comes right through to healing

and wholeness, they are likely to be totally dynamic for God. For they have found God in a place of such despair that it is beyond the imagination of most people to comprehend. Because of where they have come from, they know, without any shadow of doubt, that God is able to heal. Some know, even, that they would be dead now, were it not for what Jesus has done for them.

How it grieves their heart to hear people, who have not been deeply involved in the healing ministry, rubbishing those who have sought to rescue the sheep that were lost; or disparaging the deliverance ministry, or saying such things as *"You are a Christian now, you are a new creation in Christ, all your problems should be over."* The naivety of some people's theology and their attitude to those who are hurting is sometimes beyond belief. The same people who give the impression that a Christian should not have any problems are not slow to visit the doctor for themselves when they are in need!

There were some people who came for help in the early days of the ministry who were, themselves, pioneers. In a sense they knew their real need better than their doctors. They knew their problems could not be tackled with drug medication and they needed the help which only God could give.

One lady who had been labelled manic depressive for years, and had suffered from many other debilitating conditions, originally came to Ellel Grange because of an acute fear of spiders. God healed her of the fear through deliverance but that only served to expose much deeper needs which lay beneath the surface. One by one the problems were resolved as the Holy Spirit brought the real issues to the light, which then had to be faced and dealt with. She has now been off all medication for her former conditions for more than five years.

Another lady, with long-standing problems, was constantly encouraged by the Lord to keep on going back to Ellel Grange even though the team were not yet able to help her. But deep down she knew that one day the answer would come. Years later, after some of the team had spent many months developing their understanding about the whole area of broken personalities, they had the answers she had been waiting for. Her patience and endurance has now been rewarded. Her former problems are now things of the past.

Recently a secular psychiatrist described one of his patients as having come from a worse background than any of his other patients. He openly admitted that he could only offer heavy drug control, electric shock treatment and residence in psychiatric care. That same patient has now been completely free of all drug control for well over a year and will be able to share with her former psychiatrist how God has healed her from the inside out and put her life back together.

Healing the Broken Hearted is now the title of a special training course dealing with the issues of broken personalities, sometimes referred to by the medical professionals as Multiple Personality Disorder (MPD) or Dissociative Identity Disorder (DID). The team have seen some major breakthroughs in finding keys to help those people who have been distraught for years with the consequences of such disorders. There have been some outstanding testimonies of healing as God has restored people so that they only have the one personality that God intended them to have.

Sadly, however, some people, whose ministry experience is largely limited to deliverance, could not accept that the well-known symptoms of such disorders could be anything else but demonic and chose to distance themselves from this area of ministry. In reality demons are involved, but they are not the only problem and a much broader understanding of healing needs is essential in order to bring the very hurting and broken to a place of healing.

The lessons that have been learned in ministering to the broken-hearted, to those who have been devastated by deprivation, abuse and violence have also had far-reaching consequences in other areas of ministry. There are many people, for example, who have suffered trauma through accident to whom God has brought wonderful healing, even many years after the event, by applying the principles that have been hard-won in longer-term ministries.

The patience and endurance of those who have hung on to God as they have believed for their healing has been abundantly rewarded. Jesus told the story of leaving the ninety-nine to go after the one. It has often been the case that the lessons learnt in caring for the one have subsequently been a real blessing to a significant number of the ninety-nine!

It is not easy to be on the cutting edge, but the team have discovered the hard way, that it is the only safe place to be. They have seen first hand why it was that when Jesus came proclaiming the Kingdom of God he also healed the sick and told the disciples (the Church) to do the same. Salvation and healing are, in the Gospels, one and the same. Through the cross people can be healed (saved) for eternity. But God's love is not limited to the afterlife. Paul told us to *"work out our salvation with fear and trembling"* (Philippians 2:12) to live it in the here and now. Through the healing ministry people experience the love of God.

Ultimately, healing is simply the restoration of God's order in a person's life. For many of the hurting lambs who have found hope and healing behind the scenes at Ellel Grange, or at one of the other centres, the search for restoration of God's order in every part of spirit, soul and body has been the key that has led them on a path of restoration and hope.

As part of the pioneering programme of Ellel Ministries, specialist training and ministry courses are being developed to cater for people with particular conditions. Some of these have already progressed beyond the pioneering stage to being regular features of the Ellel programme. *Healing for Victims of Accident and Trauma* and *Ministry to the Childless* are typical examples.

A new pioneering course on cancer is under development and as the Lord leads and the team gain understanding and experience of ministering to people with this and other conditions, more such courses will be added in time.

In all these specialist ministries it has been seen how God's gift of creativity is often suppressed in the character of those who have been deeply hurt in life. A recent development in the ministry provides training in how to develop the creative side of one's personality through which God can bring deep healing.

The cost of long-term, behind-the-scenes, hospital-type ministry is, however, great. If one looked on it in National Health terms it would be completely non-viable. The long hours of work, the need for great vigilance and intensive care make this a costly ministry that is not for the faint-hearted!

One day the testimonies of those whose lives have been totally transformed by God in this sort of intensive ministry will be told in book form also. Their stories and journey with Christ to freedom and new life have been miraculous and a great inspiration to the team. The eventual fruit has far outweighed the cost.

To witness the power of Christ transforming a life from the inside out, giving worth and value, a future and a hope and a depth of relationship with Jesus which can even surpass the need for healing is the essence and heart of the work of Ellel Ministries. Notwithstanding the costs involved the Trustees of The Christian Trust believe it is right never to charge for ministry, even of this nature, leaving it up to individuals (or their Churches) to make a donation if they wish and are able to do so.

Financial provision, of both capital for expansion of the facilities and revenue for overheads, is the biggest single blockage to being able to do much more of this vital in-depth work with broken lives. The potential harvest for the Kingdom is great, but the labourers are all too few. Pray that the Lord will send out more labourers into the harvest and provide resources for the building work and the training of workers.

CHAPTER 18

The Pierrepont Vision

A living bridge to a needy world

The Vision

The vision for Ellel Pierrepont is to provide a residential college environment so that Pastors, Counsellors, Leaders etc can come from all over the world for longer term teaching, training and practical experience.

We live in an era when the world is searching for healing answers in everything from acupuncture to transcendental meditation! The world recognises that people are searching for spiritual answers for many of their inner problems, and the New Age explosion is Satan's answer to the spiritual vacuum that two centuries of rationalism, (in the western world at least), has bequeathed to humanity. Newspaper articles about well-known people being involved in New Age spiritualities and the occult have had the effect of popularising this deception and licensing it for the world at large. *"If it's OK for them it's OK for me"* is not an uncommon reaction. Sadly, as a Church, we have largely failed to teach the truth of Scripture and apply God's remedies for healing.

A similar scenario has been played out in the whole area of sexuality. Magazine after magazine headlines and glorifies the affairs of the stars, rich and famous. Uncritical media attention to their behaviour has lowered the moral threshold to such a low level that anything goes unchecked - unless of course you are a politician and political mileage can be made out of sexual indiscretion!

The real consequences of ungodly behaviour are seen day in and day out, both in the Ellel counselling rooms and the local Church. The ministry needs of the age we live in are increasing dramatically and the need for in-depth training and practical ministry experience is critical, as God gives His people the burden to bring hope to the hurting.

The 9-week Schools, shorter training courses and Healing Retreats are important elements in the Ellel Training and Ministry Programme, but for many people they are not enough.

Pierrepont Estate

The team first began to pursue the vision of a major teaching and training centre in 1992. Clarendon School in Bedfordshire had just come on the market. It was large, well-located and seemed very suitable, but before an offer could be considered the property had been sold. The team kept their eyes and ears open and the next time a potential property came on the market, they were given the information by Jill Southern, whose daughter was a former pupil of Clarendon School!

Following her positive experience of the second 9-week school at Glyndley Manor, Jill was determined to bring the Ellel teaching to her local Church and area. In February 1994, therefore, the team visited Farnham, in Surrey, for a weekend's conference. Peter and Otto Bixler were on the team.

The day before the conference Jill contacted Peter and said, *"Pierrepont School in Frensham has just come on the market, we are wondering if part of it might be suitable for our Church. With all your experience of buildings, would you be willing to have a look at it whilst you are here?"* Without too much thought Peter responded positively and said he would bring Otto with him.

Late on a wet Friday afternoon, with umbrellas up and just as the winter night was closing in, Peter, Otto and Jill ventured up the Pierrepont drive. Even though Jill lived in Frensham it was her first visit. The place seemed vast. They almost laughed at the thought that such a huge place could be thought of as being suitable as a property for Frensham Baptist Fellowship's thirty or so members!

But as they walked round the grounds and entered the main building Peter was suddenly very aware of the earlier vision for an international training centre for Ellel Ministries. *"This is it",* he thought. Privately he shared his thoughts with Otto. Otto did not disagree. The weekend conference went ahead, there was much blessing and the team went home. But they could not forget about Pierrepont - neither could Jill Southern.

The next time Jill returned to the property God showed her a unique vision of the world as a globe. The globe was rolling up the Pierrepont drive and it stopped with India at the front of the main house. In the vision a door opened and into Pierrepont walked some Indians. The globe rolled again and stopped at another country. Out walked some Africans. Eventually the globe had stopped outside all the countries of the world and nationals, often in national costume, had stepped into Pierrepont from even the farthest corners of the globe.

The conclusion of the vision was in reverse. After their time of training at Pierrepont all the people climbed back into the globe and returned to their home country. God had shown Jill that students would eventually come to Pierrepont for training from every country of the world and then return to their homelands to put what they had learned into practice. Jill was gripped by the vision and she, with her husband Ron, were ready to lay down everything to see the vision fulfilled.

At this stage in the development of Ellel Ministries there were nine people on the Executive Leadership. There was no way they could consider taking on such a vast undertaking unless every single one of the leaders were in unity about the project. They met for a special meeting at Ellel Grange. They talked, they prayed and then each spoke their heart. There were no dissenters. They believed that the vision for Pierrepont was of God, and notwithstanding the seeming impossibility of the project, they committed with Jill, and the others who were supporting her at that time, to believe for a miracle.

The property was on the market at *"offers over 1.75 million pounds"*. In addition to the magnificent old house, there were many ancillary buildings, old and new, including houses, a sports hall, a modern block of workshops that would be ideal as an administration block and a quantity of modern classrooms which could be converted into bedroom accommodation if necessary. There were sportsfields, woodlands, river, gardens and greenhouses - a vast amount of property and facilities in 35 acres of beautiful grounds. But, as usual, Ellel had no money!

Eventually an offer had to be submitted and there was both joy and apprehension when the offer of 2.1 million pounds was accepted by the vendors! There was then a time-limit on arranging the finance. Once again the vision for a development of the work was shared with supporters - especially in the South of England where Pierrepont is. But notwithstanding some very sacrificial giving, money seemed painfully slow in coming in. The amount of money being prayed for was far greater than anything Ellel had looked for before.

Amazingly, however, with the help of gifts, loans, a substantial bank mortgage arranged by one of the supporters of the project, and much prayer, the target was reached and on 14th February 1995 the deeds of Pierrepont House were handed over to Ellel Ministries - or, slightly more accurately, to the bank! What a battle it had been - and still is! The full story of all that happened then and subsequently will be told at another time.

Equipping the Property

Having bought the property it then had to be staffed and equipped. People came from all over the place to share in the vision and vast amounts of equipment were given from the most unlikely of sources such as Shell International (who gave the equivalent of a football field in area of quality carpet tiles from the Shell Building in London's Strand!) and the Ministry of Defence with whom, for the Pierrepont team, the name Tadley will be for ever indelibly associated!

Back in the seventies Barry Jay had worked for the Ministry of Defence (MoD) at Vickers in Barrow-in-Furness. Barry established a Christian Union there. One of those who attended was an MoD employee named Jim Bluck. Jim's employment with the MoD eventually came to an end and he was given living accommodation in a Ministry of Defence Hostel. Jim followed the fortunes of Ellel Ministries when Barry Jay joined the team and became a faithful and committed prayer partner of the work, coming on a number of courses.

In 1995 Jim telephoned Pierrepont one day with the news that the MoD had recently refurbished the hostel he was living in, at Tadley, about 17 miles away, but that someone in Whitehall had just made the decision to close it down. Jim was advising the team of this because he had heard the buildings might be demolished and that there would, therefore, be some equipment available. *"It might be worthwhile,"* he said, *"contacting the MoD."*

Jim left the message with the switchboard, but getting no immediate response persisted with further calls until it got to the ears of Jill who went, with another member of the team, to Tadley to investigate. What they found was exactly as Jim had said. The caretaker there advised Jill to apply to Whitehall as he had been told that the decision had been made to allow charitable organisations who were willing to provide their own labour to benefit from the decision - there were all sorts of things, from beds to buckets and sheets to showers.

The MoD were keen to get on with the job and, amazingly, gave Ellel Ministries official permission to take whatever they wanted. They did not bargain for the Pierrepont team, which had been ably supplemented by a team of volunteers who had been recruited at the Brighton Conference.

They turned up with a 17 ton truck and proceeded to strip the buildings inside and out! That truck made fifteen journeys between Pierrepont and Tadley and a rough count of what came into the work is as follows:

- 200 beds with bedding, bedroom mirrors, wardrobes, cupboards, bookshelves, curtains & bed-side cabinets
- Hundreds of electrical items including shaver sockets, strip lights, switches, sockets, cables, security lighting, lamp posts etc.
- 150 toilets and related plumbing items including baths, basins, shower cubicles, shower trays, radiators, towel rails, copper piping etc.
- Kitchen equipment including a full stainless steel kitchen, tables, sinks, fridges, griddles, ovens, hobs, refrigeration units, cold room, pots, pans, cutlery, utensils, potato peelers etc, etc.

- Dining room equipment, round tables, serving tables, trolleys, heated plates, storers, racking etc.
- Plus dozens of other miscellaneous items including carpets, doors, door locks, double glazed window units, up-and-over garage doors etc., etc!!

Just after occupying Pierrepont, the huge wrought iron gates were stolen. One of the Scriptures given to Jill at that time, by someone who did not know that the gates had just been stolen, was from Isaiah 60:11 which says, *"Your gates will always stand open, they will never be shut, day or night, so that men may bring you the wealth of the nations."* In a very real sense that 17-ton truck brought some of the wealth of the nation through the gates of Pierrepont and deposited there a massive donation from the nation's resources!

On the personnel front people came and people went. As Director of the new work Jill had to walk through the pain of seeing some of those who had committed themselves with her to seeing the project through, having to pull back for various reasons. But Jill remained rock solid in the midst of it all, hanging on to her vision of the globe and its occupants.

In addition to the ongoing series of Healing Retreats, which were started almost as soon as the ink was dry on the sale deed, it was decided that the main Pierrepont teaching programme should begin with a six month training school. Ellel had always used Luke 9:11 as a foundational Scripture for the ministry and the initial letters of Nine Eleven Training School (NETS) were adopted as a descriptive name for the training programme. So the NETS school was born. Getting the building ready for the arrival of the first students in February 1997 was an incredible achievement for the site and facilities team.

Practical Miracles

One big problem was heating the main building. The old boiler and antiquated heating system had obviously worked at some time in the distant past. But now it was long defunct. Some professional heating engineers estimated a cost of over a hundred thousand pounds to put in a new system and that was out of the question.

Could Big Bertha, as the old boiler was affectionately called, ever work again? Ian Coates and Basil Bird went to work with gallons of penetrating oil and enthusiasm, an enormous amount of toil, sweat and tears (to say nothing of the occasional drop of blood!) and gained a major victory. For the grand sum of under twenty pounds (and hundreds of hours of dedicated labour) the heating system was working again - and has run magnificently ever since, never once breaking down! This enabled the nineteenth century listed building to be brought back into use in time for the arrival of the first NETS students.

There were to be many more such miracles behind the scenes - such as provision of a car park! Pierrepont needed adequate space for visitors to park their cars. A local company quoted £40,000 for the work of excavation, putting down hardcore, levelling and tarmacing the selected area of land. There was no money for such expenditure. As the Estates Manager, Paul Graham, drove to work each day he passed a large pile of granite stones that no-one seemed to be using. One day he was prompted to knock on the door of the farm where the stones were stored to ask what they were going to be used for. The farmer told him they had been purchased as hardcore to build a new road to the farm-house, but that now they were moving house and had no further use for them. *"You can have them for nothing if you pay for the transport,"* he said!

The top soil that covered the car park was then sold and

the money obtained for the soil paid for the transportation of the stones. A roller was hired to roll them in and there was just enough to complete the job.

But what about the tarmac for the surface? A telephone call to the local authority extracted the information that just two miles away they were about to scrape the tarmac off the road surface. And, yes, the scrapings were available at £1.50 per ton delivered. The scrapings duly arrived and were rolled into the hard core to produce a road quality surface - all for less than £500 all in!

On the first NETS School there were students from fourteen different nations. They lived together, learned together, laughed together and cried together. But above all God met them on the School in a very deep way and at the end of the School there were some very remarkable testimonies of what God had done in their lives. They are now back home starting to fulfil the second part of Jill's vision. 1998 saw the completion of NETS 2 and 3.

In the lounge of Pierrepont there is a huge wall map. As students come from the different nations a flag is inserted on their country. Jill's vision is slowly being fulfilled as the flags begin to cover the world. There will be quite a celebration of thanksgiving when a flag is placed on the last country!

The development of such a major training centre is no small responsibility for such a new and pioneering organisation. But there have been many prophetic words over the years that the time is coming when Churches in the Body of Christ will be crying out for help with ministry to their people. It is the team's prayer that the training Pierrepont will be able to provide will be a strategic contribution to the global Christian community.

Another prophetic word at the beginning of the Pierrepont ministry stated that there would be two battles over

Pierrepont - the first to acquire the property and the second to keep it. The first was won and the second is being fought as the team intercede daily for the funds to service the loans.

In the meantime the blessing flowing into the Body of Christ is real and tangible. A man booked onto NETS 4 is only going to be there because of the transformation that took place in his wife on NETS 2. Together God has restored them and is now equipping them for a lifetime of service.

CHAPTER 19

Opposition, Pain and Failings
The Human Story

Whilst much of this book records some of the wonderful things that have happened during the development of the work of Ellel Ministries, it would be less than honest not to record that there has been opposition to the ministry from some quarters and that the team has had to face a variety of personal and ministry problems along the way.

It has always concerned the team, however, that those who did wish to make an issue out of something so rarely checked either the facts or visited the ministry. On three separate occasions, for example, influential antagonists went into print with disturbing comments about the work and, sometimes, the personnel, without ever having come near Ellel Grange. Specific invitations to each of them to come and assess the ministry for themselves and talk about the issues they had raised were met with neither a reply nor an acknowledgement.

Opposition has also come from some Churches who appeared to be challenged by members of their congregations receiving help from elsewhere. It is always the desire of Ellel to work with local Church leaders as far as is possible. But sometimes, when people come for help, they do ask for confidentiality. On our part, through many of the pressures of pioneering, we realise that we have not always helped those who were cautious about healing and deliverance to understand what God has been doing through Ellel Ministries.

With regard to personnel, there have been those who have joined the Staff on a full-time, part-time or volunteer basis who have subsequently left prematurely feeling negatively about the ministry. The team have no wish to use this book, or any other publication, to say to them anything other than *"thank you",* because each person *has* touched the life and the work of Ellel Ministries and brought significant blessing through their involvement. They have brought a rich variety of gifting and personality which has enhanced the whole. Each gave of themselves sacrificially and thanks are due to them for their contribution to the story of Ellel Ministries.

Over the years there have been many times when the warfare has been so intense that some wondered if either the people or the work would survive the fire! The warfare has manifested itself in both the subtle and the obvious. There have been direct media attacks, sometimes using isolated and disaffected individuals. There have been misrepresentations and complaints from some who have misjudged the heart and through hurt and pain or fear have entered into verbal campaigns.

It should never be forgotten that it is Satan who is the enemy, not people, and it is his work that must be opposed. The weapons of the flesh such as accusation, finger pointing and taking offence are deadly. If Ellel Ministries is a true work of God then He will protect and defend it, whatever Satan does to undermine and oppose it or whatever mistakes man makes through human weakness and fallibility.

At a personal level there has also been the painful human story of marriage breakdown. In the early days of the ministry Peter had to walk through the deep disappointment, sense of failure and pain of separation from his first wife and, subsequent divorce. This was a distressing time for Peter, his former wife and their two children. The issues were deep and long-standing, but at the end of the day he had to face the decision of either continuing to be obedient to the vision God had given, or to walk away from his calling and commitment to his lifework. In spite of all the pain and trauma of human failure associated with the consequences of this God continued to bless the ministry.

As the work grew and developed the team also, had to face the fact that some people, whom it was thought might be with the work for a long time, chose not to stay. It was never easy saying farewell to those who left the work. Most left for good reasons. God had called them into the ministry for only a season and then moved them on to work in another ministry or, at another place, taking with them the lessons and experience they had gained whilst being at Ellel. Most of these have remained close friends and associates of the work.

There were times, however, when people chose to leave for other reasons. For some the pace may have been too exhausting. For others God had brought issues to the surface of their lives which needed to be faced and dealt with.

Some people who joined the team, even in senior positions within the work, later found their vision not to fully coincide with the vision and aims of Ellel Ministries. Others, also, found it hard to work within a team setting or had different views on management style. For a variety of reasons, therefore, some people have left. Those things which some of them were wanting to do were not, in themselves, wrong, but God called Ellel Ministries into being for a specific purpose, and if more than one vision is trying to be worked out within the same structure the threat of di-vision is great.

In some cases, the Ellel leadership failed to make the ministry's aims and vision sufficiently clear and in consequence this in itself caused disappointment and misunderstanding, as some who joined found their expectations were not fulfilled. Tensions and strains in personal relationships inevitably arise when this happens and, with mutual understanding and forgiveness, a parting of the ways may well be the right way forward for all the parties concerned.

A lack of single-mindedness (obedience to vision) has blunted the effectiveness, and sometimes been the downfall, of some Christian ministries and the Ellel leadership has sought to remain faithful to the vision, notwithstanding many pressures to move in various other directions, which initially may have seemed attractive but, ultimately, were not felt to be in God's will for this ministry.

This is not to imply that we in Ellel Ministries have been perfect! Far from it, for there have been times when we have appeared to over-react, or to have been too dogmatic or too defensive. This may well have caused hurt to others, and where this is the case we would ask for (and offer) forgiveness and pray for reconciliation, as we continue to press on with the call God has placed on the ministry.

Keeping going in the face of all the pressures has required a tenacious walk of faith, both in respect of the intensity of personal ministries and, also, in the realm of financial provision for the work. These have often resulted in intense personal pressures, but the freedom gained for those who have been set free has been worth it all.

The learning curve the team have taken in understanding soulishness and deception has made Ellel Ministries something of an enigma. Coming from strong Bible-based and evangelical backgrounds and yet experiencing, too, the reality and freedom that comes through the Baptism in the Holy Spirit, and having to apply this in real-life situations, has brought a radical edge to the ministry, together with a deep discernment of what is false or superficial.

Neither the false nor the superficial will ever bring healing to the very broken. Eleven years of tackling and undoing Satan's work in people's lives through constant prayer, the use of Scripture and the application of the work of the cross has resulted in the team having an unshakeable belief in the truth of God's word and a real awareness that Satan hates it and opposes it to the core.

Satan will use any weakness, any sin, any chink in a Christian's armour to undermine the truth of God's word and try to bring to nought the work of those who are applying these truths in the healing ministry. The primary lessons of the journey have taught through hard experience, as opposed to theological idealism, the fact that God's power is infinitely greater than the enemy's, and His power to keep, His faithfulness, His provision, His leading and His way are all that ultimately matters.

Opposition and pain could be seen as being negative, but it is through entering the crucible that God can forge His purposes within us. Through the pain and the cost God has been found to be a powerful redeemer. Through criticism, human failure, misgivings, betrayal, judgements and accusation deep lessons have been learned, providing opportunities for a deepening of faith, repentance and of becoming more yielded to Christ.

In 1994 Peter married again. His second wife, Fiona (referred to earlier in the book), was also divorced with two children. She had experienced deep pain and rejection in the breakdown of her first marriage. God is a redeemer, however, and the healing He brought to them, through their marriage, has in itself been a picture of the reality that God is able to restore and use those who themselves have been hurt and broken.

Team members recognised that God had been drawing

Peter and Fiona together and their marriage also brought greater stability to the work as they shared together in ministry and leadership responsibilities.

Perhaps the deepest pain the team have experienced is nothing to do with any of the above, but is the spiritual pain of seeing and experiencing the depths of broken-ness in the Body of Christ through the thousands to whom the team have ministered. Their cry for help far outweighs the ability of the team to meet it and it is only through the Church being trained and equipped to minister that any realistic impact can be made into the backlog of healing needs. One can never be content with the extensive waiting lists that centres such as Ellel have.

In the Gospels, Jesus encourages us to rejoice when there are problems, when opposition mounts and when people speak less than well about you. This is one Scripture that it is never easy to endorse, though some comfort can be taken from the fact that others have walked the same path - especially in the healing ministry. It seems that Satan has a particular objection to Christians actually doing the works of the Kingdom or of them receiving healing - especially through deliverance!

So this chapter records something of the human story of walking with God on a difficult but rewarding journey. Human beings are fallen and fallible, and the story in this book is intended to be a testimony of God's love and grace and not that of human triumph or tragedy. It is not man's story, it is part of God's restoring work, and all the glory goes to Him for what He has done.

Along the way we have learned much about healing and much about ourselves. But above all we have learned about the character and mercy of God. We know that He has not finished with us yet. We look forward to all that is to come!

CHAPTER 20

Joys and Blessings

Over the years the team have been privileged to share in the enormous joy that so many have experienced as God has met them at their place of need. There can be nothing more thrilling than watching God at work in people's lives, in so many different ways.

Unto Us a Child is Born

Children are a gift from God. When a couple are unable to receive such a gift, the pain and suffering is often very deep. There are few greater joys than praying for a couple who have been unable to conceive and then hearing the news that a child is on the way. Wherever the team have visited they have prayed for childless couples, often with considerable success. Once a year there is now a special *Ministry to the Childless* course at Ellel Grange or Glyndley Manor on which the keys to healing that have been learned over the years are shared with potential parents.

One couple who came on the course returned home with the set of teaching tapes. They lent them to some friends who had been childless for eighteen years. They applied the truths that were taught on the tapes into their own lives and to their amazement conceived a child forthwith!

A Sussex couple came to a Church weekend. They had been barren for a number of years. They responded to a word of knowledge about childlessness and were prayed for. The lady was delivered from a spirit of death. Just over nine months later Hannah Elizabeth, their special gift from God, was born.

In Sweden a woman came running to the front of the meeting. She and her husband had been trying for a child for six years. She was also delivered from a spirit of death. Less than a year later Jon Olav was born. In Norway a lady was at first shocked, and then delighted, when she became pregnant at age 48 and gave birth to a daughter. She and her husband had been childless for over twenty years since the birth of their other child.

In Hong Kong a very pregnant woman came to the conference at Hang Fook Camp. She and her husband had been childless for eight years. The team had prayed for them the previous year. The consequences were very obvious for all to see! One couple came on the Childlessness course at Glyndley Manor. Almost exactly nine months later they sent a photograph of Ella - named after Ellel Ministries! She had been conceived at Glyndley Manor after her parents had been prayed for on the course!

The principles of healing are universal. They apply to human beings the world over. In the Scriptures God heard the prayer of the childless. God is still hearing and answering their cry today.

Healed Through Deliverance

In 1991 the first part of Peter's two volume book on *Healing Through Deliverance* was published. *The Biblical Basis* was followed by *The Practical Ministry* a couple of years later. These books are full of scriptural exposition as well as practical insights into ministry. Their contents are based on much practical experience. The books make it clear that deliverance is only one aspect of healing, but emphasise that without deliverance there are some people who are unable to be healed.

An eighteen year old girl waited for prayer at the Ellel Grange monthly Healing Service. When asked what her trouble was she said that her Doctors had told her that she probably had less than twelve months to live. She was like the woman in Luke 13 whom Jesus said had been bound for eighteen years. Like the lady in the Gospel, she was first delivered of a spirit before she received prayer for her healing. Over a twenty minute period of continuous prayer, the pain and swelling in her kidneys subsided. Six weeks later she wrote to say that her Doctors had re-examined her, they could not now find anything wrong with the kidneys and had told her to forget what they had told her last time and go away and live a normal life!

A sixteen year-old boy had been an epileptic since being a young child. People at Church and school all had their instructions as to what to do when James had a fit - which was regularly in spite of his medication. During a weekend visit to his Church he was found unconscious, after a fit, in the Church porch. The team prayed for him and, in particular, delivered him of any spirits that had come down the generation line. Within a few minutes he regained consciousness, sat up, stood up and was amazed at the fact that he was able to stand up and had clear vision. Normally after a fit he was unable to stand and would have double vision. He was healed of epilepsy, subsequently confirmed by the doctors at his local hospital. Seven years have passed and James has not had any more fits.

A lady was in constant pain following an accident several years earlier when she had fallen down stairs. She came on a training course and brought with her a special bed on which she had to sleep in order to hold her spine in a safe position. On the second night of the course she was delivered of a spirit that had been cursing her whole generation line. She, her mother and her grandmother had all had many accidents. After deliverance she felt God straightening her back and bringing the muscles and bones back into right alignment. That night she slept pain-free without her special bed. She visited Ellel Grange three years later and gave testimony that her back had been completely healed and that she had never needed the bed again.

Alina was Polish. She had fallen off a second floor balcony at the age of twelve. At twenty two she was in constant pain and now had a scoliosis of the spine. God not only delivered her of much demonic power that had been influencing her life since being a very young girl, but restored her body as well. Her spine was straight and her body pain free. The following day she was rejoicing at a good night's sleep. Three months later she wrote to confirm what God had done for her.

Blessings of a Different Nature

For many people Ellel Grange, or one of the other centres, or a conference has been the place where they found salvation. To find Christ as Saviour is the most wonderful and profound healing that anyone can ever receive.

In 1970 Joy, who is now an Associate Counsellor at Pierrepont, was working in Spain with Operation Mobilisation. She witnessed to, and prayed for, two young children whom she had been asked to look after. She had no idea what happened to them subsequently. But twenty seven years later, these same two children turned up at the 1997 Brighton Conference, *Equipped for a Purpose,* where Joy's prayers were answered. Amazingly, she was there to see God transform their lives.

One of them, Mandy, had already become a Christian before the Conference. She had been specially invited to the conference by a Spanish member of the team. At Brighton she was healed of eating disorders and addiction to alcohol. Her brother had not been keen on going to the conference, but agreed to try it out for one day only. God so touched him during the foundational teaching, however, that he was back the following day and stayed right through to the end.

On the second day of the conference he gave his life to the Lord. He came on the platform to testify and give thanks for what God had done for him. What rejoicing there was as Joy celebrated a twenty-seven year answer to her prayers. Since then Mandy has completed the 8-week School at Ellel Canada and her 80-year old Father, who first asked Joy to look after his children so many years ago, has also given his life to the Lord. The ramifications of praying for children can be astonishing!

A salesman came up Ellel's drive with the intention of selling double glazing to the ministry. His hopes of a big sale quickly diminished as he was told there was no money for such things. But he was given some leaflets about the ministry. Later he came to a Healing Service and was impressed by what he saw happening, so he applied to come on a Healing Retreat. On arrival, in those days, people had to complete a form saying why they had come. His form read *"To get out of double glazing into insurance!"* He had deduced that if God could heal people then a little matter like changing his job could be easily accommodated. On the second day of his retreat he got into the assurance of faith as he gave his life to Christ.

One man came on a retreat very close to death. His counsellors felt no release to pray for his healing. But they did pray into a number of issues in his life that were causing him distress. For the first time in his life he was at peace - God had healed him on the inside. Following his death his widow wrote to thank the team for what God had done through them. She said that his last two weeks were the happiest of their life.

Another man told people as he was dying, *"Don't let anyone say that God didn't heal me at Ellel Grange"*. The spiritual healing he received was so profound that it now meant far more to him than the physical healing he had sought for so long.

There is no limit to the blessings that God wants to pour out on his children. For many people the results are not instantaneous because there are issues that have to be resolved in their lives, choices which have to be made, or lifestyles that have to change. It's not unusual, therefore, for testimony letters to be received several months, or even years after a time of ministry. With the benefit of hindsight they can look back and see what God has done.

Whether the fruit is immediate or delayed, the source of the healing is always God and it is to Him that all the glory must go for what He does in bringing healing to His people.

CHAPTER 21

The Weapon of Prayer

The significance and importance of prayer in the Ellel story is incalculable. Intercessors have been asked to pray about each and every development in the ministry - both before Ellel Grange had been purchased and at every stage since.

Some of the words given by intercessors were strategic in confirming the rightness of various steps along the way. At each of the major conferences there has always been a team of intercessors who have been praying behind the scenes during every meeting. When there have been major issues or important decisions to make confidential prayer warriors behind the scenes have been at the heart of the situations as they developed.

After Ellel Grange was opened the monthly meeting for prayer became formalised as the first Prayer Support Group. This group has met every month at Ellel Grange (excepting August) for the past twelve years. It is a public meeting which is open to all who wish to come. At each meeting one of the leaders reports on what has been happening in the work during the previous month and then shares the programme for the following month. Praise, thanksgiving and detailed intercession for every aspect of the work are the only agenda at these meetings.

When Glyndley Manor was acquired, the Glyndley Team followed the same example. Now, on the same Monday night every month there are Prayer Support Group meetings at each of the five centres. Additionally there are monthly Prayer Support Group meetings in various other parts of the world as ex-students take up the call for prayer and share in the burden.

Barry and Jan Jay have been at the heart of the Ellel prayer ministry. After their three years as Wardens of Ellel Grange they took a time out to seek God afresh for their future. Three months later they were back helping Glyndley Manor get established in the south of England. Many people were praying and it was Barry and Jan who took up the vision to coordinate intercessors all over the south into a chain of monthly Prayer Support Group Meetings.

So effective were they in encouraging prayer that before long there were eighteen different groups meeting every month to pray for Ellel Ministries - in places as far afield as Tenby in South Wales, Sidmouth in South Devon and West Malling in Kent. Not infrequently people at these Prayer Support Groups brought strategic words into the ministry.

Barry and Jan had become the first Ellel Ambassadors. They carried the flag for the ministry far and wide. Especially effective was their commitment to the Ellel Stand at the annual Christian Resources Exhibitions in Sandown Park and Manchester. When Ellel Canada was opened up Joe and Ruth Hawkey followed in the steps of Barry and Jan's vision and pioneered a series of similar Prayer Support Groups across Canada.

In the North of England Bruce and Janet Edwards accepted the challenge of following Barry and Jan's example, and, as a result, stimulated prayer at the other end of the country. As a result there are now regular meetings taking place in Scotland, Northern Ireland and various places in Northern England.

The Hungarian Christians have been especially diligent in praying for the work. Two Prayer Support Groups, at opposite ends of the country, have met on a monthly basis ever since the work began in Eastern Europe. Otto and

Sharon have tried to be present at most of these meetings. A similar regular meeting now takes place in Poland.

As the work has grown in its international commitment, so the need for prayer has increased. Ever since the beginning of the work there has been a desire for twenty-four hour prayer cover for the whole ministry. At the end of 1997 this came into being, initiated by Barry and Jan Jay, and pioneered by Simon Robertson at Ellel Pierrepont. It is now to be coordinated for the whole ministry by Ros Keefe at Glyndley Manor.

On a more personal front there has always been a chain of intercessors who have accepted responsibility to pray for specific people or situations as and when the need arises. This has been especially critical in some of the behind the scenes private ministries, where, because of the need for confidentiality, it has not been possible to share the information more widely. There have been times when the intercession of these prayer partners has made the critical difference between victory or defeat.

In the early days of the ministry, when Otto and Sharon Bixler were still living in California, there was a particular ministry that was going on late into the night. The team were tired, so Peter rang Otto and, taking advantage of the eight hour time difference, asked him to pray about the situation whilst Otto was still awake. An hour later he came back with a word of knowledge about the person who was being prayed for that was either very right or very wrong! In faith they prayed about the issue that Otto had come up with. It was a word straight from heaven and proved to be a key that broke the oppression of the enemy and led to a captive being set free.

There may be a temptation to think that the larger a ministry becomes the less it needs prayer supporters. The very reverse is the truth. God does not enlarge a ministry for its own sake, but only so that it can fulfil the purposes for which He called it into being. The more effective a ministry is in fulfilling its vision, the greater will be the need for prayer.

So an enormous debt of gratitude and thankfulness to God goes to the small "army" of people who have prayed and interceded. Without them the ministry would be weak and ineffective. It has been a wonderful encouragement to see God lay prayer on many people's hearts and see this "secret" side of the work grow and blossom against all human odds!

In Ephesians Chapter 6 Paul highlights prayer as being one of the key weapons in the ongoing battle against the powers of darkness. Things have not changed. As long as Ellel, or any other ministry, is taking ground from the enemy, there will always be a critical need for intercessors to share in the battle in the heavenly places.

CHAPTER 22

Leadership, Structure and Money

Organisational History

At the end of 1987 there were 14 people working full-time within Ellel Ministries. At the beginning of 1998 there were 175! In addition to the full-time workers there are an additional 250 or so volunteer Associate Counsellors who come in on a regular basis to help with personal ministries at the five centres. Being responsible for so many people, their welfare and their income, as well as the upkeep of five centres is a very considerable responsibility. In order to cope with the developing ministry there have had to be many changes over the years in the organisation and structure of the work.

At no time has Peter wanted to operate alone as an autocratic leader. As the visionary behind the work, however, his position as overall leader has always been recognised within the ministry. He has always sought the security of mutual accountability as the Leader of the work within the structure of a leadership team. Before Ellel Grange was even opened he established both an Advisory Board, which met very regularly, and a Council of Reference of people who knew Peter and wanted to support the development of the ministry.

In the early days the Advisory Board acted very much like a non-executive management group, aiding Peter with making the major decisions. They even got involved in the interviewing and appointment of some staff, such as the first Wardens of Ellel Grange. In time some of the Advisory Board also became Trustees of the Registered Charity, *The Christian Trust,* which is legally responsible for the ministry.

The Advisory Board comprised a mixture of local leaders. Its Chairman for many years was Malcolm Colmer. Malcolm, until his recent retirement, was a Consultant Surgeon in Liverpool and he and his wife Anne had been long-standing friends of the Horrobin family, first knowing Peter as a young teenager at a Crusaders Bible Class. Ellel owes much to Malcolm's steady and encouraging hand as he steered the Advisory Board and the Leadership Team through the early years of the ministry.

Bishop Bill Flagg also played a significant role, both on the Advisory Board and as a Trustee, until he moved from the Liverpool Diocese to become General Secretary of the South American Missionary Society. Sister Aine's presence on the Board was always a joy to experience. She was full of fun and practical common sense. Nothing phased her and her faith always rose to the challenge of adventuring with God.

Don Binsted and Bobby Cooper, both of whose ages challenge the younger ones to renewed endeavours, have served within the work from its outset, right through to assuming their present roles as elder statesmen within the Ministry, still continuing to provide help and Godly advice to Peter on sensitive or difficult issues and on decision making. Don and Maddy (prior to her untimely death in 1996) and Bobby and Grace are the salt of the earth. Without their sacrificial involvement Ellel Ministries would not be what it is today.

Right from its beginning the work was also encouraged and supported by Bishop Morris Maddocks and his wife Anne. Bishop Morris was one of the major pioneers of the healing ministry within the Church of England and was responsible for establishing the *Acorn Christian Healing Trust*. He acted as a Consultant to the Advisory Board of The Christian Trust and Peter always valued his wisdom and personal advice.

A few years after the ministry was established, however, the Council of Reference was eventually disbanded as they were all very busy people and none of them were ever able to visit Ellel Grange to see for themselves what God was doing. Their role as a reference point for the work had become limited.

Eventually, also, it became unrealistic for most members of the Advisory Board to be closely involved in the management and development of the ministry. There was too much going on for a non-executive body to be fully effective. The full-time team had to assume responsibility for the day-to-day running of the work and an Ellel Grange Leadership Team evolved - a pattern which has subsequently been followed at the other centres. Each of the centres now has a local Leadership Team which has autonomous responsibility for running the work in accordance with specified overall guidelines for the ministry.

Leadership and Structure

The overall leadership of the work is now in the hands of a group which is referred to as the Executive Leadership. Peter is the International Director of the Ministry and the other members of the Executive all have key roles within the work. Fiona Horrobin carries the overall brief on the Executive for Ministry, Anna Wood is responsible for Personnel. Philip Moore is the Trust Corporation Secretary. Otto Bixler is the Director of Operations in Eastern Europe, Donna Parachin is the Director of Ellel Canada, David

Cross is the Director of Glyndley Manor, Jill Southern is the Director of Ellel Pierrepont and Ken Hepworth is the Director of Ellel Grange. Under Peter's leadership, these nine people carry the spiritual responsibility for the development and running of the work.

Support and Advisory Group

Outside the work the Executive Leadership is supported by a Support and Advisory Group (SAG) which aims to meet twice a year with the Executive and is available at other times to provide advice, support and help to Peter and the other Leaders where relevant and necessary.

Bishop Graham Dow has been on SAG since its inception. Ellel Ministries made two Church visits to Holy Trinity, Coventry for local teaching conferences during Bishop Graham's time there as Vicar. Bishop Graham is one of the very few senior clergy in the Church of England with a practical understanding of deliverance as well as having a considerable amount of relevant experience. We are very grateful to him for his support at considerable personal cost.

The story is told elsewhere in this book of how Chua Wee Hian, the well known Bible expositor and Pastor of the Emmanuel Evangelical Church which meets at the Emmanuel Centre in Marsham Street, Westminster, became associated with the work. He is a man who also has extensive overseas experience with the International Fellowship of Evangelical Students. Gordon Clarke is a former educational psychologist who is now involved in full-time Christian counselling with Christian Fellowship Ministries in the North East of England. He has been associated with the work since before Ellel Grange was purchased.

Rev. Jim Graham is very well known as an outstanding Bible teacher and is now Pastor Emeritus of Gold Hill Baptist Church. Rev. Chris Woods is the Vicar of Holy

Trinity, St Helens. Chris has known Peter since their Mission England days and has been involved in the healing ministry for many years. David Noakes is a former lawyer with a very acute mind and a deep understanding of Scripture and has a well-recognised prophetic and teaching ministry.

All of these are busy people with significant ministries in their own right. Their commitment to the work through their involvement on the Support and Advisory Group is deeply appreciated by every member of the team.

The Registered Charity

The deeds of the original registered charity proved an inadequate instrument for the management of the developing ministry, so *The Christian Trust* was incorporated as a new Trust Corporation, a company limited by guarantee, in 1994. At the end of 1997 there were four Trust Corporation Directors, all of whom are members of the Executive Leadership.

In 1992 a separate limited company was established in order to carry out the commercial aspects of trade in books and tapes. Ellel Ministries Limited ploughs all profits from the sale of books and tapes back into the ministry and tithes its gross profit to other Christian causes.

The work in Hungary is organised in a similar way. A limited company owns the land and property and a registered charity runs the ministry. In Canada a separate Canadian Charity is legally responsible for both the ministry and commercial aspects of running the work.

Philip Moore is the Trust Corporation Secretary and does an outstanding job in ensuring that all the legal requirements of the ministry, and its associated companies, are carefully adhered to. Philip was formerly in banking before taking early retirement and originally served the

Trust as its first Bursar. He is one of those loyal, committed and dedicated people without which an organisation such as Ellel Ministries would be unable to function.

Money and Friends!

Ellel has never been an affluent organisation. It has always existed in that very narrow strip of Christian territory lying between need and surplus. Usually the balance has been tipped on the side of need! Nevertheless, even though some bills have been paid late and there has had to be dependence on bank support, every bill has always been paid and the ministry is able to look back with much thanksgiving to God for the way He has provided - often in quite extraordinary ways.

The nominal financial support received by YIPS is referred to elsewhere. The rest of the team are offered a series of optional allowances (such as for personal living costs, housing, car, holiday etc) according to their need and length of service within the work. No-one receives anything near a commercial salary and some of the team contribute to the ministry by declining to take any allowances, trusting God for their provision from personal supporters, pensions or other private sources. For everyone on the team it is a walk of faith requiring a regular commitment to pray in the money for their allowances.

Right at the beginning of the work the Lord made it clear that those who come for personal ministry, whether for a short personal appointment or a residential stay on a Healing Retreat, should never be charged. There is an opportunity on each retreat for people to make a donation if they wish, but, on average, such donations contribute no more than about a third of the real cost.

What is learnt in personal ministry is taught on the Training Courses, so the courses, for which people do pay, are an important source of income for the whole ministry. The largest element in the income is, and always has been, from personal donations. Some people give occasional gifts, while others contribute regularly every month as members of the *Friends of Ellel Ministries*. Each of the centres runs its own Friends scheme. Each Friend is committed to supporting the work on a regular basis in terms of both prayer and giving.

In common with most Christian ministries, Ellel has, from time to time, gone through periods of particular financial difficulty. It is at these times that the Lord has occasionally moved one or more individuals to give a significant amount. The timing of some of these gifts has often been quite extraordinary as God has prompted people to give just the right amount at the time of greatest need.

At the beginning of 1997 the Executive Leadership faced an especially difficult situation, with major bills and allowances to pay and no money with which to pay them. Otto described the situation to the team on a Monday morning in February as a spiritual siege and asked them to pray that the siege would be broken. On the Tuesday the Executive Leadership met and spent much of their meeting interceding, as they brought the situation before the Lord.

On the Wednesday evening the spiritual siege became physical as masked robbers invaded Glyndley Manor and attempted to rob the empty safe. No-one was hurt but a new Polish YIP was put up against a wall and was initially terrified, thinking she was going to die. Then the Lord showed her all the promises he had given her for her life and realised that most of them were yet to be fulfilled so she wasn't going to die and need not be concerned! The raiders fled empty handed.

Then on the Thursday morning Philip Moore opened a letter from a person who had been in previous correspondence with him about making a donation. Philip had no idea how much the donor was thinking of. He could hardly believe his eyes as he pulled a cheque out of the envelope for £50,000. Three weeks later the same donor was to give a further and similar amount. The siege had in fact been broken, and in a quite extraordinary way. What rejoicing there was as the team gave thanks to God for His deliverance and mercy.

Ellel Ministries is not only a pioneer work, but it is also a faith venture in which the team are totally dependent on God to meet the needs through the generosity of His people. Apart from special situations such as the above, the amount of money coming in to each centre on a regular basis is usually just about enough to cover the costs and overheads of the work. But the need to repay existing bank borrowings, incurred at times of major expansion of the work, is now a major prayer target for the ministry.

As an organisation the work of Ellel Ministries is now more like a missionary society, with teaching and ministry opportunities, as well as financial commitments, in many parts of the world. The work in Eastern Europe and Russia, the training of leaders from third world nations, teaching conferences in Africa are all examples of vital ministry operations that, without funding, can only remain at a standstill. These, and many other cries for help that Ellel receive stretch faith and resources to their absolute limit!

CHAPTER 23

The Wider Vision of
Ellel Ministries

In 1997 a large team, mainly of Staff and Associate Counsellors, visited the Ukraine. Kremenchug, where the main teaching conference was held, is the principal town in the region of Poltova. Poltova was one of two regions in the former Soviet Bloc where the authorities experimented with destroying every Church building and either shooting or sending to Siberia all the Church Leaders. The Church was driven underground but, in secret, it thrived and since the communist walls came down Christianity in the region has flourished, notwithstanding the continuing oppressive influence of the former communist authorities.

God blessed the people at this conference in an extraordinary way, and not just in the area of healing. It was a time when people grew in faith and understanding as many of them heard foundational Christian teaching for the first time. For these people Christ has been all they had and they had found him to be sufficient for every need. They have much to teach us in the West about trust and dependency on God.

Not only did they understand the teaching, on topics such as forgiveness and establishing Godly order in our lives, but they gladly applied it into their own lives. It is not surprising, therefore, that there was so much healing taking place in the meetings. Wherever there has been genuine repentance, God's anointing for healing has been at its greatest.

After the conference the team broke up into six groups who conducted mini-conferences in different regions of the Ukraine. On his way back to England Peter visited a large Church in Kiev. After he had finished preaching, at the second service of the morning, he was about to leave the Church on the way to the airport when Pastor Anatoly called him back on to the platform.

In his hand he held a long box. As he opened it Peter's eyes fell on the most beautiful piece of cut glass he had ever seen. It was a long crystal horn, modelled after the horn in the Old Testament that was used for anointing with oil. As Pastor Anatoly held the horn in front of him he looked at Peter and said, *"We want you to have this as a gift to Ellel Ministries. We want it to be a reminder to you that God has poured much into Ellel Ministries and we would ask you not to forget to keep on pouring it out for the Body of Christ around the world."* His words had a profound effect on Peter and in some ways he returned from the Ukraine a different person.

He had been freshly challenged by the whole vision that God had given him for Ellel Ministries. While healing was important, the vision was much broader than just healing. It was for the whole message of the Kingdom which does, of course, embrace healing and deliverance. On his return to England, Peter scoured the Gospels afresh for a deeper understanding of Jesus's teaching on the Kingdom of God or the Kingdom of Heaven. At the Brighton Conference in November 1997 Peter focussed special attention on teaching about living in the Kingdom as a result of his Ukraine experiences.

It was as if during the first ten years of the ministry God had been establishing a strong foundation for a credible ministry that had brought together the proclamation of the Kingdom, healing and deliverance, in much the same way as they might have been seen in the Gospels. But now God was saying you have to take this message to the world - to wherever you are invited and whenever God opens the doors. Whilst, through the various Training Schools, this was already happening, after the Ukraine there was a new sense of urgency in Peter's heart - as if he had been made freshly aware of the days in which we live and that time is short.

Much of the Church may not want to hear such a message, but the whole Ellel Ministries team is committed to teaching and training so that the Body of Christ will be equipped for the purpose for which God called it into being. The world in which we live is moving very fast. New Age beliefs and practices have invaded every sector of society - from the offices of management consultants to the private lives of famous and infamous world personalities - and also infiltrated some Churches

Millennium fever seems to have gripped the world - without much thought for the fact that the millennium is not just the passing of a random date but the marking of 2000 years since the first coming of Jesus. Much of the Church is in deep division over multi-faith issues, the new age, matters of sexuality, the existence or otherwise of Satan and hell, foundational doctrines such as the Virgin Birth, the sinlessness of Christ and, even, the fact of the resurrection - largely because some Church leaders no longer adhere to the truth and authority of the Scriptures.

In the work the team have found that it is only by being faithful to the teaching of Scripture that people are able to enter fully into healing and be set free from the powers of darkness. When Jesus said *"the truth shall set you free"* (John 8:32) he was not postulating an optional theory of religion, but speaking out the reality of the fact that *in Him, and only in Him, can be found the keys to life.*

Those with other beliefs, or no belief, may find the words of Jesus in John 14:6 *(I am the way, the truth and the life. No-one comes to the Father except through me)* less than palatable, but it is only because of this abiding truth that during the first twelve years of Ellel Ministries many, many hundreds of people have either found faith in Christ for the first time or have been healed or delivered.

Truth, by definition, is unchanging. Jesus is the same, yesterday, to-day and for ever and the commission He gave to the Church remains unchanged, *"Go into all the world and make disciples ..."* Disciples are those who do what the teacher has taught them to do. Doing the works of the Kingdom remains the vision and calling of Ellel Ministries.

Past students of the training schools are serving the Lord in every continent of the world. Each has taken with them the commission that Jesus gave to the whole of the Church for the whole of time - to preach the Gospel, heal the sick and to cast out demons. This is a commission that will not change until Jesus comes again. Right round the world God's Spirit is moving on His Church to equip and train the Body of Christ to do the works of the Kingdom and follow in the steps of the first disciples.

None of us know what lies ahead, but we do know that only in Christ is there any eternal security. The schools are part of the discipling process of helping people to receive healing from their past so that they can walk forward into the future that God has prepared for them.

The continuing goal and aim of Ellel Ministries is to be a resource to the Body of Christ and a servant to the local Churches as we take part in sharing in the fulfilment of the Great Commission. Please pray for the team as they press on with their unfinished task.

Significant Events in Ellel's History

1986

April

16th — Contracts signed for the purchase of Ellel Grange and deposit given

16-31 Oct — 198 Days in which 90,000 brochures, 20,000 mini leaflets and 20,000 Newsletters were distributed

May

19th — First meeting of the new Advisory Board

October

5th — Special Gift Day for the purchase of Ellel Grange

31st — Completion of purchase of Ellel Grange and the Chapel

November

5th — Vineyard Ministry Team use Ellel Grange as accommodation for Lancaster Mini Conference. Otto and Sharon Bixler's first contact.

15th — First Monthly Prayer Support Group at Ellel Grange including Open afternoon and Thanksgiving Celebration (700 attended)

1987

January

6th — Barry and Jan Jay started as the first Wardens of Ellel Grange

13-17 — First *Healing Retreat* at Ellel Grange

24th — First 1 day Training Course - Over 200 people attended, *Getting Acquainted with the Healing Ministry*

February

6-8 — First *Associate Counsellors Training Weekend*

16th — First *Healing Service*

March

2-4 — First residential course at Ellel Grange *Moving on in the Healing Ministry*

May

20-23 — First stand at Christian Resources Exhibition, Sandown Park.

June

13th — First Open Day

September

14-16 — *Healing for the Church of Christ* Paul and Gretel Haglin's first visit to Ellel Grange

October

19-22 — First *Deliverance Ministry Training Course*

30-31 — *Distributing the Power* First Anniversary Conference at Lancaster University

1988

April

26 & 29 — *Christian Set Yourself Free* Graham Powell's first visit to Ellel Grange (Marquee)

September

19-21 — *Transformation of the Inner Man* John & Paula Sandford's first visit

October

14-15 — Leaders Day Conferences - Bill Subritzky's first visit (Marquee)

28-29 — *Commissioned to Serve* Second Anniversary Conference at Lancaster University

April
25-27   *Healing the Inner Man* - Paul and Gretel Haglin's first visit
May
27-2 June   *Youth Leaders Workshop* and Evangelistic Meetings
               with Eric Delve (Marquee)
June
2nd   Purchase of Redwards Old People's Home completed. Property
               renamed King's Lee.
9th   *Bringing in the Kingdom*
               Tom Marshall's first visit to Ellel Grange (Marquee)
September
5-7   50th Healing Retreat at Ellel Grange
22 & 25   *Healing Through Deliverance* - Peter Hobson, Australia

February
12-15   **The Battle Belongs to the Lord**
               First UK National Conference at the Brighton Centre
June
8-10   *Men of a Different Spirit.* Bob Gordon's first visit to Ellel Grange
July
7-10   First visit to **Eastern Europe**
               Peter Horrobin & Joe Hawkey go to **Romania**
28-8 Aug   First *Holiday Weeks* at Ellel Grange
October
2nd   Otto and Sharon Bixler join the team from California
26-27   *See His Glory.* Fourth Anniversary Conference at Lancaster
               University with Marilyn Baker and Wellspring. (Vision for the
               purchase of Glyndley Manor first shared at *See His Glory*)

February
1st Week   Prayer Tower restoration finished
13-19   **Gibraltar & Spain:** Team visit to Peter Armon & Horizons
March
14-18   **Norway:** Church visit to Bergen
18th   Prayer Tower is commissioned and dedicated
April
27th   First *Prayer Support Group* at Glyndley Manor
June
               Healing Through Deliverance (Volume 1) published
1st   Ellel Ministries Ltd incorporated as a separate company to handle
               book and tape sales. The name of the work changed from Ellel
               Grange to Ellel Ministries
10-13   **The Battle Belongs to the Lord**
               Second UK National Conference at the Brighton Centre
17-21   **Hungary: The Battle Belongs to the Lord** - Budapest
               First Hungarian Conference translated into 7 languages
August
29-30   First *Team Conference*
October
               Canada: *Deliverance Ministry Training Course*
               at Singing Waters Retreat Centre, Orangeville.
December
16th   Purchase of Glyndley Manor completed.
               Joe and Ruth Hawkey appointed as first Directors.

February

8-11 April   *School of Evangelism Healing and Deliverance*
First 9 week School at Glyndley Manor

17th   Otto and Sharon Bixler set off for Hungary to establish a base

March

17-19   First *Healing Retreat* at Glyndley Manor

April

First *Prayer Support Group* in Budapest

13-16   **Canada:** *Deliverance Ministry Training Course*
at Toronto Airport Vineyard

June

8-11   **Hungary: *The Battle Belongs to the Lord***
Second National Conference in Hungary

12th   **Hungary:** *Ur Retje* first discovered

14-21   Follow on visits to **Lithuania** (Vilnius), **Estonia** (Tallin), **Ukraine**
(Komjata) and **Hungary** (Ujszasz)

July

14-16   100th *Healing Retreat* at Ellel Grange

25-29 Aug   Glyndley Manor's first *Holiday Schools*

September

17th   First Meeting of *Support and Advisory Group* (SAG)

March

17th   Special Ministries Unit opened in King's Lee - Ellel Grange

April

7-14   First *Easter Holiday School* - at Ellel Grange

May

Sweden: Christian Healthcare and Counselling Conference
at The Arken Bible School, Stockholm

29-4 June   **Hungary: *The Anointing of God*** - 3rd Conference in Hungary

June

6-12   **Russia: *The Battle Belongs to the Lord*** in St. Petersburg
First Ellel Ministries event in Russia

18-5 July   **Malaysia:** *Deliverance Ministry Training Course*
at Rawang, near Kuala Lumpur

July

Dry rot discovered at Glyndley Manor

24-31   First *Summer Holiday School* at Ellel Grange

26th   Contract signed for 1st parcel of land (Ur Retje)

September

Canada: *The Battle Belongs to the Lord*
at Toronto Airport Vineyard
First *Prayer Support Group* at Debrecen (Hungary)

October

Canada: Singing Waters Retreat Centre, Orangeville becomes Ellel
Ministries North American Base. Joe and Ruth Hawkey appointed
as first Directors

1st   Tom Marshall died

26-29   ***The Church Ablaze***
Third UK National Conference at the Brighton Centre

November

16-18   *Foundations for the Healing Ministry*
First 3 day course at Ellel Canada

January

| 10-15 | **Sweden:** *Ministering to the Sexually Abused & Deliverance Ministry Training Course.* Arken Bible School |
| 31st | **Canada:** First *Prayer Support Group* at Ellel Canada |

April

	First *Prayer Support Group* for Pierrepont
7-10	**Sweden:** Christian Healthcare and Counselling Conference at The Arken Bible School (Stockholm)
8-10	**Canada:** First *Healing Retreat* at Ellel Canada

June

| 19th | **Hungary:** Site and Facilities Team went out to Ur Retje to build the Watchman's House |

July

1-3	**Singapore:** *The Battle Belongs to the Lord*
7-9	**Malaysia:** *The Battle Belongs to the Lord,* Full Gospel Assembly in Kuala Lumpur
14-16	**Malaysia:** *The Battle Belongs to the Lord,* in Sabah
18-1 Aug	**Hong Kong:** First team visit to Hong Kong

August

| | Steve Hepden becomes Director of Ellel Grange |

September

(early)	**Hungary:** Watchman's House occupied on Ur Retje
2nd	Executive Leadership commit to buying Pierrepont
30th	Exchanged contracts for Pierrepont

October

| 17-20 | **Hungary:** *A Full Life in Christ* - 4th Conference in Hungary |
| 24 - 27 | **Poland:** *The Battle Belongs to the Lord* First Polish Conference at Wroclaw |

November

	Pennant Jones becomes Director of Glyndley Manor
	Ellel Polska established
29-1 Dec	50th *Healing Retreat* at Glyndley Manor

January

6th	First *Associate Counsellors Training Day* at Pierrepont
14-18 Mar	**Canada:** *School of Evangelism Healing and Deliverance* First 9 week School at Ellel Canada
17th	New Charitable Company, a Trust Corporation, but still called The Christian Trust, took over from the original Charity
23-25	*Living in Wholeness* - First 3 Day Course at Pierrepont
24-30	**Sweden:** Church Visit to Ostersund

February

| 15-28 | **India:** *The Battle Belongs to the Lord* Team Visit to India (Dehra Dun) |
| 14th | Purchase of Ellel Pierrepont completed |

March

	Canada: Ken Hepworth becomes Director of Ellel Canada
3-15	**Ireland:** First team visit to Ireland (North and South)
28-20	150th *Healing Retreat* at Ellel Grange

April

| | *Healing Through Deliverance* (Volume 2) published |
| 22-27 | **Italy:** First team visit to Senise, Southern Italy |

May

2-5   ***The Day of His Power***
Fourth UK National Conference at the Brighton Centre

June

25th   Jill Southern becomes Director of Pierrepont

July

5-15   **Hong Kong:** Healing Conference with Jackie Pullinger-To
at Hang Fook Camp

July

16 & 19   **Kuala Lumpar** - meetings
29-5 Aug   *Healing - The Jesus Model*
First German language Holiday School at Glyndley Manor

August

28th   **Hungary:** First Dig for building the Ur Retje Ministry Centre

September

1st   Jim Russell takes over as Director of Ellel Grange

October

12-20   **South Africa:** First Pioneer team visit
31-3 Nov   ***Into All the World*** - Fifth UK National Conference
(with Jackie Pullinger-To and Chua Wee Hian)

November

3-5   Pierrepont's first *Healing Retreat*
13-17   **Poland:** *The Anointing of God* - Wroclaw
20-24   **Ukraine:** ***The Battle Belongs to the Lord***
First Conference in the Ukraine (Svetlovodsk)

1996 January

10-15   **Malaysia:** Kuala Lumpur - Team Visit
15-22   **Malaysia:** *Wholeness for Broken Lives* - Sabah

February

28-8 March   Pioneer *10 Day Healing Retreat* at Ellel Grange

March

28-31   **Switzerland:** *Healing, Deliverance and Evangelism*
First Ellel Conference in Weinfelden

June

3rd   First Prayer and Fasting Day at Ur Retje

July

27-3 Aug   *Healing - The Jesus Model*
First French language Holiday School at Glyndley Manor

September

12-14   **Australia:** *Jesus Frees*
First Ellel Conference at Melbourne, Australia
16-19   **Australia:** *Evangelism Healing and Deliverance*
Health Care in Christ Conference at Merroo, Sydney
12-28   **India:** Team visits to Madras
12-30   **Poland:** Team visit
12-30   **Lithuania:** Team visit
27-29   **USA:** First Teaching Conference in Detroit

October

31   10th Anniversary Thanksgiving for Ellel Ministries

February

1-14 July	First *NETS School* at Pierrepont
	Luke Nine Eleven Training School (NETS 1) - Begins
17-25	**Bolivia:** Martin Frankena visits from Ellel Canada
	First Ellel Ministries visit to South America

March

	Donna Parachin becomes Director of Ellel Canada
24th	David Cross becomes Director of Glyndley Manor

April

24th	Ellel Ministries Internet Web Site opened
23-27	**Denmark:** *The Challenge of Healing in Today's World*
	First Ellel Conference in Denmark

June

20-2 July	**Ghana:** *The Power to Heal, Deliver and Restore Today*
	First Ellel Team Visit and Conference to Ghana (Accra)
9-13	**Ukraine:** *The Anointing of God*
	Second Ukraine Conference in Kremenchug, Poltova
14-20	**Ukraine:** Follow on visits within the Ukraine to Kiev, Svetlovodsk,
	Kremenchug, Komsomolsk & Poltava

July

5-18	**Canada:** *The Ellel School of Healing*
	First 2 week school at Ellel Canada

September

1st	Ken Hepworth becomes Director of Ellel Grange

October

2-5	**Canada:** *The Battle Belongs to the Lord,* Orangeville

November

5-8	**Switzerland:** *The Battle Belongs to the Lord* - Weinfelden
12-15	*Equipped for a Purpose*
	Sixth UK National Conference at the Brighton Centre

December

3-6	**Australia:** *Evangelism, Healing and Deliverance*
	Second Health Care in Christ Conference, Sydney
8-10	**Australia:** *Healing the Broken Hearted*
	Specialist teaching conference, Melbourne
16-18	100th *Healing Retreat* at Glyndley Manor

April

28-30	200th *Healing Retreat* at Ellel Grange

May

15-23	**South Africa:** *Healing Through Deliverance*
	Teaching conferences at Cape Town, Durban and Johannesburg.
21-24	**Germany:** *Healing in God's Presence*
	First conference in Germany. Held in Uelsen, NW Germany

June

10th	**Hungary:** Power supply installed at Ur Retje
23rd	*Love in His Eyes* by Karen David
	Ellel Music's first Ministry Songs cassette released
26-28	*God's Creativity in You*
	First pioneer course on healing through creative arts

September

10-13	**Canada:** *The Church Ablaze,* Orangeville
	The Ellel Story published!

Training Courses
& Healing Retreats

An Analysis of Training Courses &
Healing Retreats held in Ellel Centres (1986 - 1998)

TRAINING COURSE TITLES	EG	GM	PP	EC	Total
Acceptance and Belonging (Part 1)	1	1			2
Acceptance and Belonging (Part 2)	2				2
Aiming for Spiritual Maturity	1				1
An Encounter with God	4				4
Anger - How do we handle it?	2				2
Anointed for Power	1				1
Basic Principles for Caring and Counselling	1	1			2
Battle for the Soul	5	4		1	10
Breaking Strongholds			1		1
Bringing in the Kingdom	1				1
Building a Ministry Team in the Local Church	4	3		2	9
Called to Minister				1	1
Called to be a Holy People	1				1
Called to Counsel?	6	3		1	10
Calling and Work of a Christian Leader	2				2
Challenges to the Truth of Jesus		1			1
Christ is Risen	1				1
Christian Set yourself Free	3				3
Church Leaders' Retreat	2				2
Claiming the Ground	6	3			9
Coping with Failure	2	1			3
Counselling the Terminally Ill and Bereaved	4				4
Counselling Skills (1)			2		2
Counselling Skills (2)			3		3
Counselling Skills (3)			1		1
Deliverance Ministry Training Course	24	7		7	38
Developing Gifts in the Healing Ministry	5	4		4	13
Developing Your Prophetic Gifting	1		1		2
Discernment and Deception	1				1
Discipleship Day	5				5
Discovering the Power of Prayer	1				1
Dynamic Living (1)			1		1
Dynamic Living (2)			1		1
Dynamic Praying	4	3		2	9
Dynamic Christian Living	2	1			3
Easter Healing School	2			1	3

TRAINING COURSE TITLES	EG	GM	PP	EC	Total
Effective Prayer		1			1
Emotional Freedom		1			1
Emotional Wholeness	8	4			12
Equipped to Heal				1	1
Equipped to Serve	1	1			2
Evangelism and Healing	2	2			4
Family Fellowship Week		1			1
Family Growth	1				1
Fear			11		11
Feed My Lambs, Feed My Sheep		1			1
Foundation for Healing Abused People	3	3			6
Foundations for the Healing Ministry	4	2		2	8
Foundations for Wholeness				1	1
Foundations for Christian Counselling	4	3		1	8
Freedom from Stress and Anxiety	3	2		3	8
Freedom from Fear	6	3		4	13
Freedom in Christ	4	1			5
Freedom from Backache	1	1			2
Freedom from Addiction	2	3			5
Effective Prayer		1			1
Family Dynamics		1			1
Getting Acquainted with the Healing Ministry	19	3			22
Growing in Your Healing				3	3
Healing The Broken Hearted	3	1	3		7
Healing The Inner Man	1				1
Healing Relationships within the Family		1			1
Healing from Spiritual Abuse	2	3		2	7
Healing Through Deliverance	9	6		6	21
Healing Through Deliverance for Men	3	1		3	7
Healing Through Deliverance for Women	3	2		2	7
Healing the Rejected			1		1
Healing Workshop	1				1
Healing - The Jesus Way	1				1
Healing and Prophecy	3	2		2	7
Healing - The Jesus Model (German)		1			1
Healing - The Jesus Model (French)		1			1
Healing	9	3			12
Healing and Suffering			1		1
Healing for Abused People		2		1	3
Healing Victims of Sexual Abuse				1	1
Healing for Victims of Accident and Trauma	2	2		2	6
Healing for our Children		1			1
Healing for the Church of Christ	1				1
Healing for Women		3			3
Healthy Kingdom Living		1			1
Holiday Week	7				7
Hope for the Hurting (1)			1		1
Hope for the Rejected			1		1
How to Minister to the Wounded	1				1
Inner Healing Counselling	14	2			16
Inner Healing and Emotional Wholeness	9	7	1	10	27
Inner Wholeness		1			1
Inner Healing		1			1

TRAINING COURSE TITLES	EG	GM	PP	EC	Total
Inner Healing and Deliverance (German)		1			1
Intercession and Spiritual Warfare	3	2			5
International Discipleship and Evangelism School		1			1
Intimacy with God		1			1
Introduction to the Healing & Deliverance Ministry			1	1	2
Introduction to the Deliverance Ministry	5	3			8
Keys to Wholeness		1			1
Leaders Day (Conference)	2				2
Leaders' Retreat	6	6		6	18
Learning About Healing		1			1
Learning to Pray	10	2			12
Lifestyle in Christ Discipleship Course			2		2
Living in the Power of God			1		1
Living in Wholeness	2	1	1		4
Men of a Different Spirit	1				1
Ministering to the Rejected	3	3		3	9
Ministering to the Sexually Abused	11	9	1	3	24
Ministering into the Occult				2	2
Ministering to Children	1			3	4
Ministering to the Abused	1			1	2
Ministers and Wives Retreat	6				6
Ministry to Men	1				1
Ministry to the Childless	3	1		1	5
Ministry to Marriage	6	13		11	30
Moving on in the Healing Ministry	13		1		14
Moving Under the Anointing of the Holy Spirit	13	7	1	3	24
Moving under the Anointing of the Holy Spirit (German)		1			1
Moving on in the Gifts of the Holy Spirit			1		1
NETS (6 Months School)			3		3
New Age and Alternative Medicine	1				1
Obsessions and Phobias	1				1
Pastors and Leaders Conference	3			2	5
Personal Transformation		1			1
Post Deliverance After Care Course	3				3
Power for Healing			1		1
Praise and Worship in Spiritual Warfare		1			1
Praise and Worship Workshop		1			1
Preparation for Marriage	6				6
Preparing a Person for Healing and Deliverance		1			1
Preparing for Revival the Lasts	1				1
Principles of Leadership		1			1
Realising Godly Dreams and Visions	1		1		2
Realising your Spiritual Potential	1	1			2
Rebuilding Life after Failure	1				1
Rejection and How to Overcome It	8	5		7	20
Relationships		1			1
Resting in God's Love	1				1
Restoring the Family			1		1
Restoring the Rejected	5	3			8
Resurrection Power	1	1			2
Right Relationships		1			1
School of Evangelism, Healing and Deliverance (9 Weeks)		8		4	12
Setting Children Free	3				3

TRAINING COURSE TITLES	EG	GM	PP	EC	Total
Specialist Aspects of Healing & Deliverance	4	2		1	7
Spiritual Warfare and Claiming the Ground				2	2
Spiritual Warfare and Intercession for Women				3	3
Spiritual Protection			1		1
Spiritual Warfare	6	3	1		10
Stress, Accident and Trauma			1		1
Stress and Anxiety			1		1
The Perfume of God's Anointing	1				1
The Fire and the Flame	1	1			2
The Ellel School of Healing (Part 1)				1	1
The Prophetic Ministry	2	1			3
The Power of the Blood of Jesus	1				1
The Word and The Spirit		1			1
The Anatomy of Healing	1				1
The Calling and Work of Christian Leader	2				2
The Christian's Promised Land	2	1			3
Transformation of the Inner Man	1				1
Understanding Prophecy			1		1
Understanding Non-Christian Religions	1				1
Understanding Relationships			1		1
Understanding the Cross			1		1
Understanding Living in Wholeness			1		1
Understanding the Character of God			1		1
Understanding the Holy Spirit			1		1
Understanding Deliverance			1		1
Understanding Deception	2	1		1	4
Understanding Acceptance and Belonging			1		1
Understanding Inner Healing			1		1
Understanding Dynamic Praying			1		1
Understanding God's Power	2				2
Understanding Godly Sex and Sexuality	5	5	1	3	14
Using the Gifts of the Holy Spirit	2	1			3
Walking into Life		1			1
Walking in the Anointing	3	1		1	5
Walking in your Healing		4	1		5
What Now Lord?	2			·	2
When we don't Understand what God is doing			1		1
Women in Warfare			1	1	2
Worship Workshops			1		1
Worship with Wellspring	1				1
Worship	1				1
Young People's Week		1			1
Youth Leaders Workshop	2				2
Youth Weekend	1				1
TOTALS	**387**	**208**	**62**	**124**	**781**

HEALING RETREATS	EG	GM	PP	EC	Total
1 Day Healing Retreat	54	1			55
3 Day Healing Retreat	204	111	37	60	412
10 Day Healing Retreat	1				1
TOTALS	**252**	**106**	**30**	**57**	**468**

Please note: All figures correct to date of publication